KB270099

50 Poems

by Yoon Dong-ju

for Learners of Korean

한국어 학습자를 위한 윤동주 시 50선

> ### *Tradition is not the worship of ashes,*
> ### *but the preservation of fire.*
>
> Gustav Mahler

'전통'이란 조상이 남긴 보물을 숭배하는 것을 넘어, 그 조상이 가슴에 품었던 열정을 시간이 지나도 꺼지지 않도록 지키는 것이라는 의미입니다. 윤동주는 세계의 근대 역사가 이룬 문학의 성과를 한글로 계승하고 한반도의 지역적 한계를 극복하려고 노력한 아름다운 청년입니다.

한국어 학습자를 위한 윤동주 시 50선은 윤동주의 시 가운데 50편을 골라서 시에 등장한 문법 및 표현을 바탕으로 한국어 1급에서 4급(A1~B2) 수준에 맞게 제시하여 시를 감상하면서 한국어 학습을 할 수 있도록 기획한 교재입니다. 이 책으로 혼자 한국어를 공부하려는 학습자를 위하여 시에 쓰인 문법 및 표현에 대한 설명과 연습 문제, 모범 답안을 충분히 담았습니다. 시의 창작 배경을 새로이 알고 아름다운 삽화로 시의 분위기를 감상하는 것은 이 책을 읽는 또 다른 재미가 될 것입니다.

시 본문과 주요 어휘, 문법 및 표현에 대한 설명과 연습 문제 지시문을 모두 영어로 번역함으로써 한국어 학습자가 윤동주 시와 한국어 표현을 쉽게 이해할 수 있도록 도왔습니다. 그리고 시를 들으면서 주요 표현에 집중하는 능력을 기르고 시의 아름다운 운율을 느낄 수 있도록 전문 성우의 목소리로 녹음한 시를 QR 코드를 스캔하여 직접 들어 보실 수 있습니다.

윤동주가 너무 이른 나이로 별이 된 지 80주년이 되는 특별한 올해를 기념하고자 하는 다락원 한국어출판부의 뜻과 윤동주 시인을 존경하는 저의 마음이 닿아 이 책이 탄생하게 된 것은 결코 우연이 아닐 것입니다. 아름다운 청년 윤동주와 그의 시를 전 세계에 널리 알리고자 하는 사람들이 모여 기꺼이 삽화를 그리고, 아름다운 목소리로 시를 읽고, 애정을 담아 글을 쓰고, 편집에 애를 썼습니다. 이 정성 어린 선물이 독자들 마음에 들기를 바랍니다.

2025년 9월

김성숙

So goes the saying. The meaning of "tradition" goes beyond admiring the treasures that our ancestors left behind, to protecting the passion that lived in those ancestors' hearts so that even as time passes, it will not be extinguished. Yoon Dong-ju is a beautiful young man who attempted to pass down the feats of literature accomplished by the modern history of the world through Hangeul, and overcome the regional limits of the Korean Peninsula.

50 Poems by Yoon Dong-ju for Learners of Korean is a textbook designed by selecting 50 of Yoon Dong-ju's poems and, based on the grammar and expressions that appear within, presenting them at Korean levels 1 through 4 (A1 through B2), so that learners can study Korean all while appreciating the poems themselves. This book is filled with ample explanations of the grammar and expressions in the poems, practice questions, and sample answers, for learners who wish to study Korean alone. It's also full of beautiful illustrations and background information about the creation of the poems, so that learners can approach from a cultural standpoint in addition to studying the language. There's another kind of fun to be found in appreciating and analyzing the poems in three dimensions.

Explanations and instructions for practice questions about the main text of the poems, as well as the main vocabulary, grammar, and expressions, are all translated into English, to assist Korean learners in easily understanding Korean and Yoon Dong-ju's poetry. And by scanning a QR code, you can hear the poems yourself, recorded by professional voice actors, so that as you listen to the poems, you can also improve your ability to focus on the major expressions used within, and appreciate the lovely rhythms.

It's no coincidence that this book was created with the will of Darakwon's Korean Book Publishing Department to commemorate this special year, which marks the 80th anniversary of the passing of Yoon Dong-ju at too early an age, and my own heart, full of respect for the poet. People who hope to spread awareness around the world of that beautiful young man, Yoon Dong-ju, and his poems all gathered happily to pour their effort into drawing illustrations, reading poems out loud, writing passages, and editing. I hope that this heartfelt gift will please readers.

September, 2025

Kim Sungsook

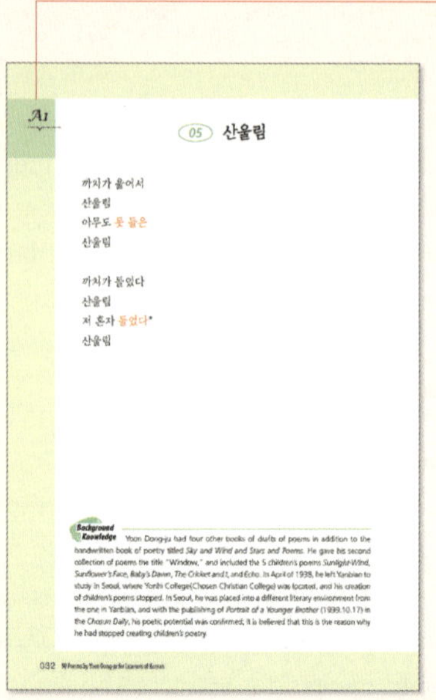

A1, A2, B1, B2는 CEFR(Common European Framework of Reference for Languages)의 등급이며, 한국어 등급으로는 각각 1, 2, 3, 4급에 해당합니다.

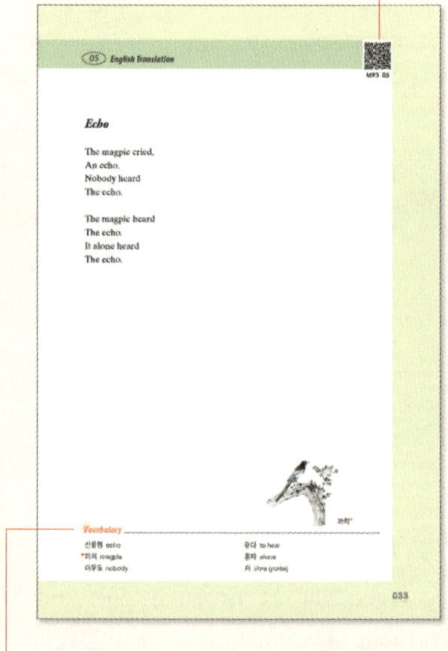

QR 코드를 통해 전문 성우가 낭독하는 시 전문을 들을 수 있습니다. 학습자는 녹음된 시를 눈으로 따라 읽으면서 듣기, 읽기 연습을 할 수 있습니다.

모르는 단어는 바로 찾아볼 수 있도록 본문에 등장한 주요 어휘를 번역과 함께 제시하였습니다. 이를 참고하여 각자 자기만의 윤동주 시 번역에도 도전해 보세요.

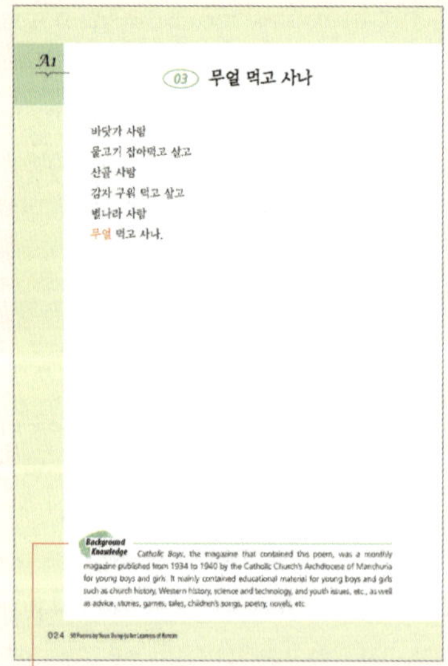

당시 윤동주의 생활상이나 시대적 배경 등 참고 지식을 제시하여 윤동주의 시를 처음 읽는 한국어 학습자의 이해를 도왔습니다.

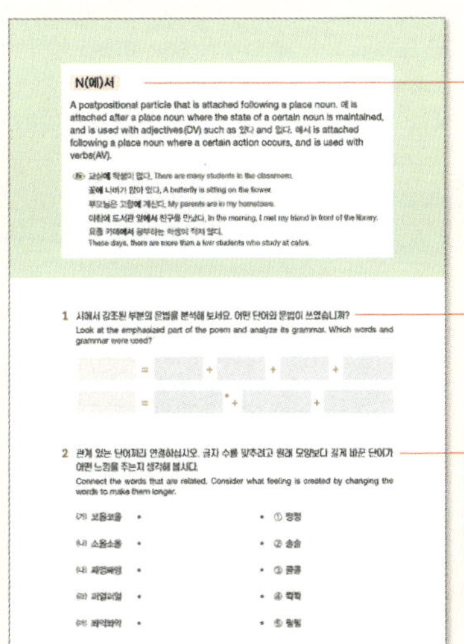

시에 등장한 문법 및 표현에 대한 설명과 예문입니다.

V: 동사, 형용사 통칭
AV: 동사
DV: 형용사
N: 명사

문법 설명 한국어 번역본은 부록에서 확인할 수 있습니다.

연습 문제를 통해 공부한 문법과 표현을 연습합니다.

1번 문항은 시 본문에서 주황색으로 표시된 부분을 형태소별로 분석해 보는 연습입니다.

2번 문항은 1번 문항에서 분석한 문법과 표현을 적용하여 문장을 작성해 보는 연습입니다.

3번 문항은 각 시에서 새로 배운 문법 및 표현 혹은 시를 읽고 난 감상을 풀이하는 활동입니다.

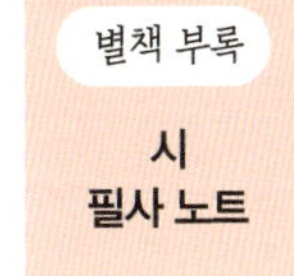

시에서 추가로 설명이 필요한 문법은 ＊로 표시해 두었습니다. 추가 문법이나 시에서 사용된 수사법에 관한 추가 설명도 제공되기 때문에 한국어 실력과 시에 대한 이해도를 동시에 높일 수 있습니다.

부록

- **모범 답안**
  연습 문제 1, 2번에 대한 모범 답안

- **문법·해설 번역**
  문법 설명과 Grammar Tip, Rhetoric Tip에 대한 한국어 번역

- **어휘 색인**

＋ 별책 부록

**시
필사 노트**

How to Use This Book

A1, A2, B1, and B2 are levels in the Common European Framework of Reference for Languages (CEFR), and correspond to Korean levels 1, 2, 3, and 4.

You can listen via QR code to a professional voice actor recite the full text of the poem. Learners can practice listening and reading while following along.

The main vocabulary that appears in the text has been presented along with translations, so that you can immediately look up words that you don't know. Try referencing this information to do your own translations of Yoon Dong-ju's poems.

Reference information has been presented about Yoon Dong-ju's life at the time, historical background, etc., to help improve the understanding of learners who are reading Yoon Dong-ju's poems for the first time.

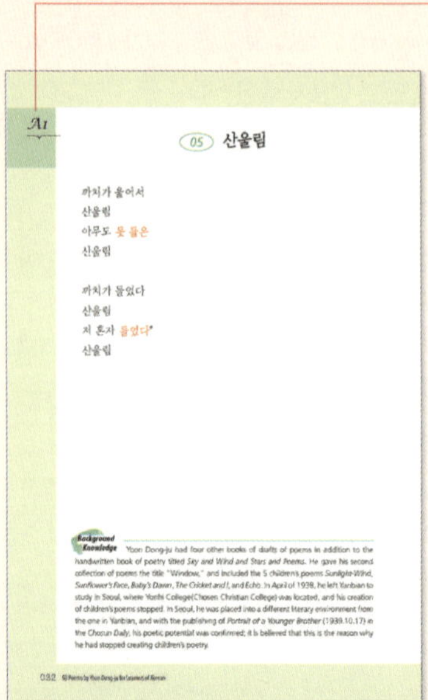

A1

05 산울림

까치가 울어서
산울림
아무도 못 들은
산울림

까치가 들었다
산울림
저 혼자 들었다*
산울림

Background Knowledge Yoon Dong-ju had four other books of drafts of poems in addition to the handwritten book of poetry titled *Sky and Wind and Stars and Poems*. He gave his second collection of poems the title "Window," and included the 5 children's poems *Sunlight-Wind, Sunflower's Face, Baby's Dawn, The Cricket and I,* and *Echo.* In April of 1939, he left Yanbian to study in Seoul, where Yonhi College(Chosen Christian College) was located, and his creation of children's poems stopped. In Seoul, he was placed into a different literary environment from the one in Yanbian, and with the publishing of *Portrait of a Younger Brother* (1939.10.17) in the *Chosun Daily,* his poetic potential was confirmed; it is believed that this is the reason why he had stopped creating children's poetry.

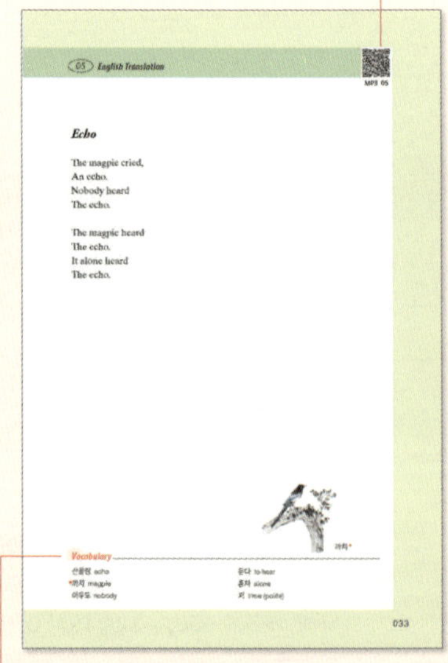

05 *English Translation*

MP3 05

Echo

The magpie cried,
An echo.
Nobody heard
The echo.

The magpie heard
The echo.
It alone heard
The echo.

까치*

Vocabulary

산울림 echo	듣다 to hear
*까치 magpie	혼자 alone
아무도 nobody	저 I/me (polite)

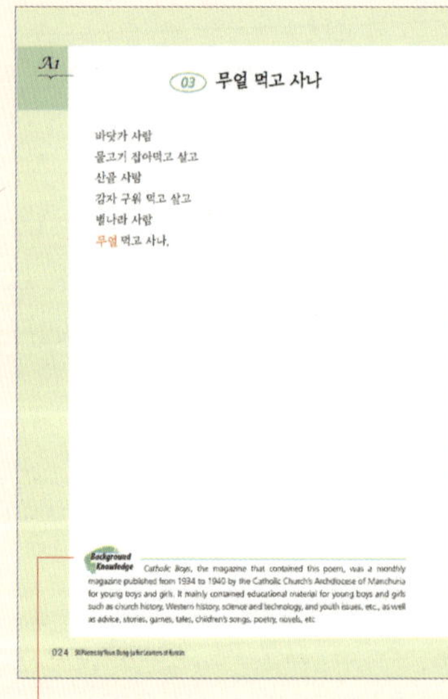

A1

03 무얼 먹고 사나

바닷가 사람
물고기 잡아먹고 살고
산골 사람
감자 구워 먹고 살고
별나라 사람
무얼 먹고 사나,

Background Knowledge *Catholic Boys,* the magazine that contained this poem, was a monthly magazine published from 1934 to 1940 by the Catholic Church's Archdiocese of Manchuria for young boys and girls. It mainly contained educational material for young boys and girls such as church history, Western history, science and technology, and youth issues, etc., as well as advice, stories, games, tales, children's songs, poetry, novels, etc.

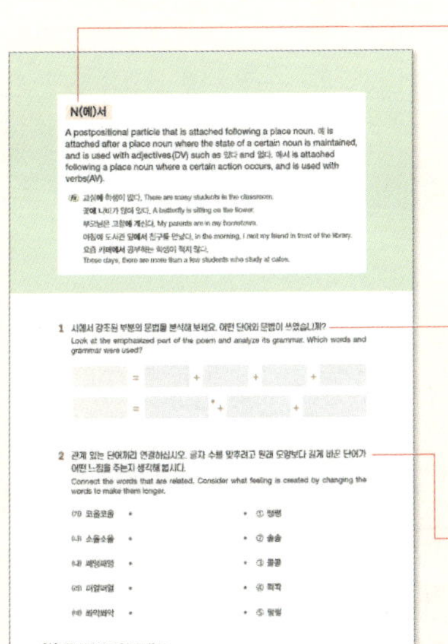

Explanations and examples of grammar and expressions that appear in the poem.

V: Verbs and Adjectives
AV: Action Verbs
DV: Descriptive Verbs (Adjectives)
N: Nouns

Grammar Explanation Korean translation can be found in the appendix.

Practice the grammar and expressions you've studied using practice questions.

Question 1 practices analyzing by morpheme the section of the text marked in orange.

Question 2 practices writing sentences by applying the grammar and expressions analyzed in question 1.

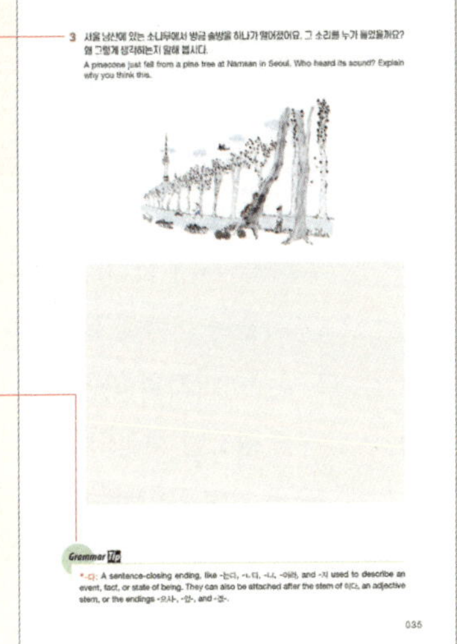

Question 3 is an exercise exploring the newly learned grammar and expressions from each poem, or the impressions gained after reading the poem

Grammar from the poem that requires additional explanation has been marked with *.
Detailed explanations about additional grammar or rhetoric devices used in the poem are also provided, so that you can improve your Korean proficiency and understanding of the poem all at once.

Appendix

- **Model Answer**
  Model Answers for Practice Questions 1 and 2

- **Grammar & Explanation Translations**
  Korean translations of Grammar explanations and Grammar and Rhetoric tips

- **Index**

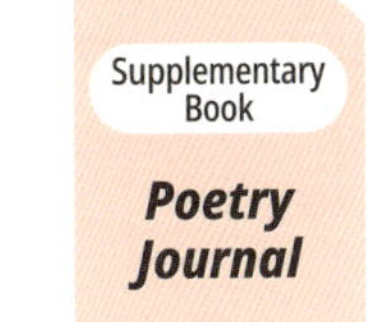

　윤동주는 1917년 12월 30일 중국 북간도에서 태어났다. 윤동주의 증조
할아버지는 1886년부터 북간도에 거주한 민족주의 지식인이고, 그의 외
삼촌인 김약연은 한학(漢學)자이자 독립 지사였다. 기독교 집안에서 자라
서 언더우드(Horace Grant Underwood)라는 선교사가 만든 기독교 학교
인 연희전문학교(현 연세대학교)를 다닌 윤동주는 어릴 때부터 기독교 문
화가 친숙했다.

　윤동주의 아버지 윤영석은 김약연의 누이동생인 김용과 1910년 결혼하
고 명동학교에서 교사로 일했다. 그리고 아이들에게 '해환, 달환, 별환'이라
는 아명을 지어 불렀는데, 장남인 윤동주의 어린시절 별명인 '해환'에는 해
처럼 환히 빛나라는 염원이 담겨 있었다. 정기적으로 출간되는 어린이 잡
지들을 구독해 볼 수 있을 만큼 경제적으로 여유가 있었던 유년시절의 그
는, 아버지의 바람대로 해처럼 밝고 성품이 착한 아이로 자랐다.

　청소년 시절의 윤동주는 학교 축구선수로 뛸 만큼 활동적이었고 재봉질
을 하여 유니폼에 이름을 새길 정도로 손재주가 뛰어났으며 교내 웅변대회
에서 1등을 할 정도로 말솜씨가 좋았다. 또한 기하학 등 수학을 잘했고 그
림에도 소질이 있었다. 만 17세 생일을 앞둔 1934년 크리스마스 이브 때부
터 그는 시를 작성하고 날짜를 적어 보관하면서 시인의 꿈을 키웠다. 그 날
짜가 적혀 있는 시는 <초 한 대>, 1934년 12월 24일이라고 적혀 있다. 그
는 김동환, 정지용, 백석, 이상의 시와 소설 작품 등을 스크랩하여 정독하
거나 필사했으며 세계문학전집을 일본어판으로 읽었다. 용정 외가에서 동
요 시인 강소천을 만나기도 했었는데, 이것이 윤동주의 동시 창작에 영향
을 미쳤을 것이다.

윤동주가 대학에서 문학을 전공하겠다는 의지를 밝혔을 때 그의 아버지는 반대하였다. 기독교 신앙을 가진 의사가 되어서 아픈 사람을 치료하는 것이 당시에 더 안전하고 실용적인 진로라고 생각했던 것이다. 하지만 윤동주는 떼를 써서 할아버지의 허락을 받아 냈고 문학을 전공하러 서울로 유학을 떠났다. 연희전문학교에서 문학을 전공하면서 최현배, 이양하 등 당대 유명한 학자들로부터 한글 정신, 세계 문학, 기독교 신앙 등에 대해서 배우고 자신의 심정을 아름다운 시어로 쓰는 연습을 했다. 그리고 프랑스어를 독학하면서 릴케, 발레리, 지드, 키에르케고르 등의 작품을 열중하여 읽었다. 윤동주가 살던 시기는 한자 대신 한글을 사용하고자 하는 정신이 확산되고 있었다. 이런 분위기 속에서 윤동주는 한글로 시를 쓰는 것을 인생의 목표로 삼았다.

일본 후쿠오카 형무소에서 숨을 거둔 윤동주는 중국 길림성 연변조선족자치주에 있는 용정 교회 묘지에 안장되었다. 중국 연변에 방치되어 있던 그의 묘지를 1985년 처음으로 발견한 사람은 일본 와세다 대학교의 오오무라 마스오 교수이다. 오오무라 마스오 교수는 윤동주의 시를 읽고 그를 존경하게 되어 윤동주에 대한 기록과 주변 증언을 토대로 수풀 아래 방치된 윤동주의 묘비석을 찾아냈다. 그 이후로 윤동주의 시는 일본에 더욱 널리 소개되었고 현대에는 남한과 북한, 일본, 중국은 물론 영어와 불어 등으로도 번역되어 전 세계에서 사랑을 받고 있다.

Yoon Dong-ju was born on December 30, 1917, in North Gando Province, China. His great-grandfather was a nationalist intellectual who had lived in North Gando since 1886, and his maternal uncle, Kim Yak-yeon, was a scholar of Chinese classics and an independence activist. Yoon, who grew up in a Christian household and attended Yonhi College(Chosen Christian College, now Yonsei University), a Christian school created by the missionary Horace Grant Underwood, became familiar with Christian culture at an early age.

Yoon Dong-ju's father, Yoon Yeong-seok, married Kim Yong, the younger sister of Kim Yak-yeon, in 1910, and worked as a teacher at Myeongdong School. He called his children by the childhood nicknames "Haehwan(bright sun)," "Dalhwan(bright moon)," and "Byeolhwan(bright star)," with "Haehwan," the nickname belonging to the eldest son, Yoon Dong-ju, containing a wish for him to "shine as brightly as the sun." In his youth, when he was financially able to subscribe to the children's magazines regularly published, he grew up as his father wished: a good-natured child as bright as the sun.

As a teenager, Yoon Dong-ju was active enough to be a soccer player for his school. Additionally, he was good enough with his hands to sew, stitching his name on his uniform himself, and spoke well enough to win first place in a speech contest at school. He was also good at math, including geometry, and had a talent for drawing. On Christmas Eve in 1934, just before his 17th birthday, he began dreaming of becoming a poet, writing poems and storing them with the date written on them. The poem written on that date, December 24, 1934, is *A Single Candle*. He made clippings of poems and novels by Kim Dong-hwan, Jeong Ji-yong, Baek Seok, and Yi Sang, carefully reading or transcribing them, and read the complete collection of world literature in Japanese. In Yongjeong, near his mother's family home, he met the children's poet Kang So-cheon, an event which may have had an influence on Yoon at the time.

When Yoon revealed his intent to major in literature at college, his father opposed him. He believed at the time that becoming a Christian doctor who treated the sick was a safer and more practical career. But Yoon pleaded for and received his grandfather's permission, and left for Seoul to major in literature. While majoring in literature at Yonhi College, he studied under prominent and famous scholars of the time, such as Choi Hyeon-bae and Lee Yang-ha, learning the spirit of Hangeul, world culture, Christian beliefs, and more, and practiced writing poetry with his own beautiful sentiments. He also taught himself French, reading with passion the works of Rilke, Valéry, Gide, Kierkegaarde, and more. At the time when Yoon lived, the spirit of using Hangeul instead of Chinese characters was spreading, and it was within this atmosphere that he wrote his poems in Hangeul.

Yoon Dong-ju, who passed away in a prison in Fukuoka, Japan, was buried in a cemetery at Yongjeong Church in Yanbian Autonomous Prefecture, Jilin Province, China. The first person to discover his grave in 1985, which had been left neglected in Yanbian, was Professor Omura Masao of Waseda University in Japan. Professor Omura had read Yoon's poems and come to respect him, and, based on records and surrounding testimony about Yoon, found his gravestone, which had been abandoned under some brush. After this, Yoon's poems became introduced more widely in Japan, and today, have been translated into English, French, and more, and are loved in South Korea, North Korea, Japan, China, and all around the world.

Contents

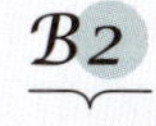

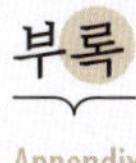

A1

봄1

못 자는 밤

무얼 먹고 사나

나무

산울림

⟨01⟩ 봄 1

우리 애기는
아래 발치에서 코올코올

고양이는
부뚜막에서 가릉가릉

애기 바람이
나뭇가지에 소올소올

아저씨 햇님이
하늘 한가운데서 째앵째앵

MP3 01

Spring 1

The baby,
At our feet, snoring, snoring

The cat,
Beside the stove, purring, purring

A slight breeze
Blowing through the branches, gently, gently

Mister Sun
Shining in the middle of the sky, brightly, brightly

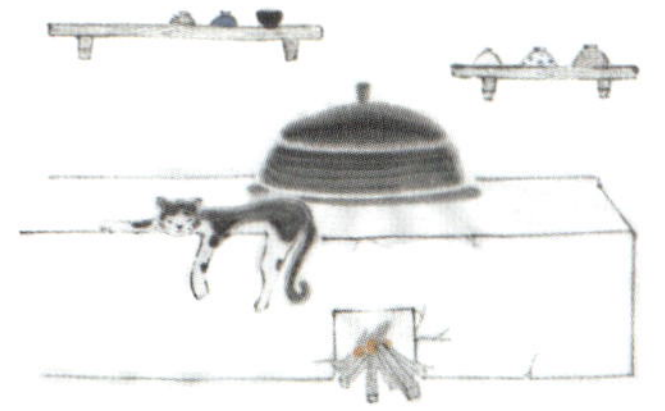

Vocabulary

발치 bottom, toward one's feet
*부뚜막 (wood-burning) stove
한가운데 the middle

나뭇가지 tree branch
햇님 the sun, Mr. Sun

N(에)서

A postpositional particle that is attached following a place noun. 에 is attached after a place noun where the state of a certain noun is maintained, and is used with adjectives(DV) such as 있다 and 없다. 에서 is attached following a place noun where a certain action occurs, and is used with verbs(AV).

(Ex) 교실에 학생이 많다. There are many students in the classroom.

꽃에 나비가 앉아 있다. A butterfly is sitting on the flower.

부모님은 고향에 계신다. My parents are in my hometown.

아침에 도서관 앞에서 친구를 만났다. In the morning, I met my friend in front of the library.

요즘 카페에서 공부하는 학생이 적지 않다.
These days, there are more than a few students who study at cafes.

1 시에서 강조된 부분의 문법을 분석해 보세요. 어떤 단어와 문법이 쓰였습니까?
Look at the emphasized part of the poem and analyze its grammar. Which words and grammar were used?

	=		+		+		+	
	=		* +			+		

2 관계 있는 단어끼리 연결하십시오. 글자 수를 맞추려고 원래 모양보다 길게 바꾼 단어가 어떤 느낌을 주는지 생각해 봅시다.
Connect the words that are related. Consider what feeling is created by changing the words to make them longer.

(가) 코올코올 •　　　　　　　　• ① 쨍쨍

(나) 소올소올 •　　　　　　　　• ② 솔솔

(다) 째앵째앵 •　　　　　　　　• ③ 콜콜

(라) 퍼얼퍼얼 •　　　　　　　　• ④ 쫙쫙

(마) 쫘악쫘악 •　　　　　　　　• ⑤ 펄펄

3 '봄'이라는 계절을 생각하면 어떤 단어들이 생각나나요? 그 단어들이 가진 봄의 느낌을 생각나는 대로 써 봅시다.

What words come to mind when you think of the spring season? Write down the feelings of spring that those words bring to mind.

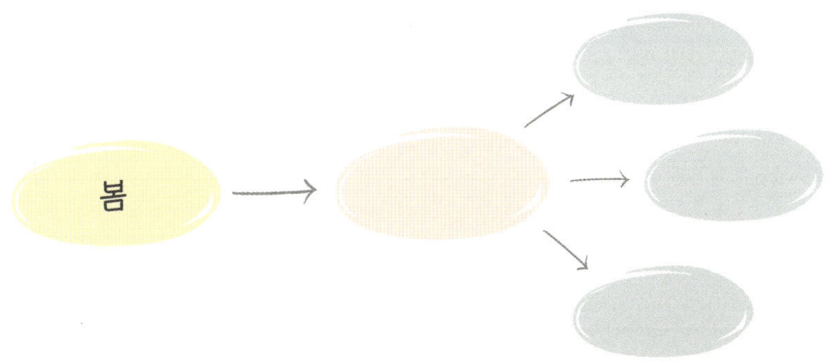

02 못 자는 밤

하나, 둘, 셋, 넷
....
밤은
많기도 하다.

못 자는 밤

MP3 02

Sleepless Nights

One, two, three, four
....
These nights
Are many indeed.

-도 하다

Attached to the stem of an adverb or adjective to express wonder or surprise. When attached to the end of an adjective stem, the nominal ending 기 is added and used as -기도 하다, or 도 is added after the adverbial suffixes -이 or -게. Like in the sentences "둘이서 저녁을 많이도 먹었구나.(Only two of you ate so much for dinner.)" and and "아이가 참 슬프게도 운다.(That child is crying so sadly.)," several other verbs instead of 하다 can also be used following 도.

Ex 밥을 많이**도** 하셨네요. You made so much food.

시간이 빨리**도** 갔네요. Time went so quickly.

말을 참 재미있게**도 한다**. You're so very fun to talk to.

머리를 참 예쁘게**도** 잘랐네요. They cut your hair so prettily.

어머니는 마음이 참 넓기**도 합니다**. My mother has such a very broad mind.

1 시에서 강조된 부분의 문법을 분석해 보세요. 어떤 단어와 문법이 쓰였습니까?

Look at the emphasized part of the poem and analyze its grammar. Which words and grammar were used?

2 관계 있는 표현과 단어를 연결하고 다음 표현을 써서 문장을 완성하세요.

Connect the expressions and words that are related and write out the phrases to complete the following sentences.

DV기도 하다

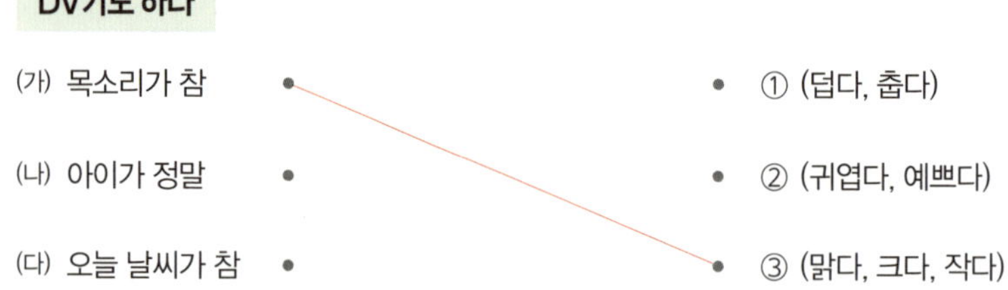

(라) __________, 네 통, … 메일함에 메일이 참 • • ④ (오래, 하다)

(마) 한 시간, __________, 세 시간 … 게임을 참 • • ⑤ (빨리, 늘다)

(바) 열 명, __________, 서른 명, … 공연장 입구에 사람이 참 • • ⑥ (많이, 쌓이다)

(가) 목소리가 참 맑기도 하다. / 크기도 해요. / 작기도 하네요.

(나) ____

(다) ____

(라) 한 통, 두 통, 세 통, 네 통, , … 메일함에 메일이 참 많이도 쌓였다.

(마) ____

(바) ____

3 어떻게 하면 밤잠이 잘 오나요? 잠을 잘 잘 수 있는 비결을 소개해 봅시다.
What can you do to sleep well at night? Introduce your secrets for sleeping well.

03 무얼 먹고 사나

바닷가 사람
물고기 잡아먹고 살고
산골 사람
감자 구워 먹고 살고
별나라 사람
무얼 먹고 사나.

Background Knowledge *Catholic Boys*, the magazine that contained this poem, was a monthly magazine published from 1934 to 1940 by the Catholic Church's Archdiocese of Manchuria for young boys and girls. It mainly contained educational material for young boys and girls such as church history, Western history, science and technology, and youth issues, etc., as well as advice, stories, games, tales, children's songs, poetry, novels, etc.

MP3 03

What Do They Live Off Of?

People by the seaside
Live off of the fish they catch,
And people in the mountains
Live off of the potatoes they roast,
So what do people of the heavens
Live off of?

Vocabulary

굽다 to roast
잡아먹다 to catch and eat
바닷가 the seaside
물고기 fish

산골 the mountains
감자 potato
별나라 the heavens, the world of stars

Instead of following a noun ending in a vowel with the object marker 을/를, an object can be marked by just attaching ㄹ. However, in reports or official writing, this shortened form is not used.

(Ex) 누굴 who / 어딜 where / 무얼 what / 그걸 that

점심은 어떤 **걸**로 할래? What do you want to do for lunch?

1 시에서 강조된 부분의 문법을 분석해 보세요. 어떤 단어와 문법이 쓰였습니까?

Look at the emphasized part of the poem and analyze its grammar. Which words and grammar were used?

	=	+	

2 다음 표현을 써서 문장을 완성하세요.

Write out the following expressions and complete the sentences.

나	너	그것	누구	무엇	어디

누구 + 을/를   [보기] 누굴

(가) ______누구______, 어제 ______누굴______ 만났어?

(나) ______________, 사랑해. ______________ 떠나지 마.

(다) ______________, 한식은 ______________ 제일 좋아해?

(라) ______________, 이걸 치우고 ______________ 이쪽에 놓자.

(마) ______________, 서울에서 ______________ 먼저 가 보고 싶어?

(바) ______________, 엄마가 ______________ 얼마나 좋아하는지 알아?

3 여러분의 고향에는 어떤 특산물이 있어요? 어릴 때부터 어떤 음식을 먹었는지 생각해 봅시다.

What are some local specialties in your hometown? Think about the things you've eaten since you were a child.

04 나무

나무가 춤을 추면
바람이 불고

나무가 잠잠하면
바람도 자오.

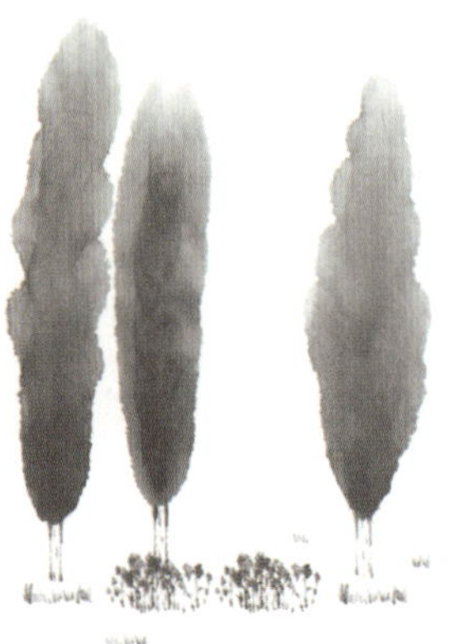

Background Knowledge

The fun in the poem *Tree* comes from reversing the scientific cause-and-effect relationship. A tree shakes because the wind blows, but the 20-year-old poet's thought that the wind blows because a tree dances is an interesting one. The poet, who yearned for independence, believed that in order for the great wind of liberation to rise, each person had to take action instead of staying quiet.

MP3 04

Tree

As the tree dances,
The wind blows,

And as the tree sleeps,
The wind sleeps, as well.

Vocabulary ____

춤을 추다 to dance (a dance)   잠잠하다 to be calm, to be quiet, to be still
바람이 불다 for the wind to blow

V1(으)면 V2

When making an assumption about an uncertain situation or when you want to say that something happens only in a particular situation, you can use -(으)면 to limit something to that situation.

Ex 비가 오**면** 등산을 안 갈 거예요. If it rains, I won't go hiking.

기분이 좋**으면** 노래를 부릅니다. When I'm in a good mood, I sing songs.

저는 점심을 먹**으면** 항상 산책을 합니다. When I eat lunch, I walk for about 30 minutes.

한국말을 잘하게 되**면** 한국 회사에서 일하고 싶어요.
When I speak Korean well, I want to work at a Korean company.

1 시에서 강조된 부분의 문법을 분석해 보세요. 어떤 단어와 문법이 쓰였습니까?

Look at the emphasized part of the poem and analyze its grammar. Which words and grammar were used?

	=		+	
	=		+	

2 다음 표현을 써서 문장을 완성하세요.

Write out the following expressions and complete the sentences.

____________(으)면 ____________고 ____________(으)면 ____________습니다.

(가) 바람이 불다 / 나무가 춤을 추다 / 바람이 자다 / 나무도 잠을 자다

(나) 꽃이 피다 / 아가씨가 오다 / 꽃이 지다 / 아가씨도 가다

(다) 아가씨가 오다 / 꽃이 피다 / 아가씨가 가다 / 꽃도 지다

(라) 비가 오다 / 고양이가 숨다 / 눈이 오다 / 산새가 숨다

(마) 고양이가 숨다 / 비가 오다 / 산새가 숨다 / 눈이 오다

(바) 나뭇가지에 해가 걸리다 / 낮이 되다 / 나뭇가지에 달이 걸리다 / 밤이 되다

(가) 바람이 불면 나무가 춤을 추고 바람이 자면 나무도 잠을 잡니다.

(나) ____

(다) ____

(라) ____

(마) ____

(바) ____

3 근처 제일 가까운 나무로 가서 바람을 느껴 보세요. 거기서 이 시를 읽는 모습을 영상으로 찍어서 SNS에 올려 봅시다.

Try going to the closest tree nearby and feel the breeze. Record a video of yourself reading this poem there and upload it to social media.

Vocabulary

해 sun	달 moon
걸리다 to hang, to be hung	근처 nearby, neighborhood
낮 day	영상 video

(05) 산울림

까치가 울어서
산울림
아무도 못 들은
산울림

까치가 들었다
산울림
저 혼자 들었다*
산울림

Background Knowledge   Yoon Dong-ju had four other books of drafts of poems in addition to the handwritten book of poetry titled *Sky and Wind and Stars and Poems*. He gave his second collection of poems the title "Window," and included the 5 children's poems *Sunlight·Wind*, *Sunflower's Face*, *Baby's Dawn*, *The Cricket and I*, and *Echo*. In April of 1938, he left Yanbian to study in Seoul, where Yonhi College(Chosen Christian College) was located, and his creation of children's poems stopped. In Seoul, he was placed into a different literary environment from the one in Yanbian, and with the publishing of *Portrait of a Younger Brother* (1939.10.17) in the *Chosun Daily*, his poetic potential was confirmed; it is believed that this is the reason why he had stopped creating children's poetry.

MP3 05

Echo

The magpie cried,
An echo.
Nobody heard
The echo.

The magpie heard
The echo.
It alone heard
The echo.

까치*

Vocabulary ________________________________

산울림 echo   듣다 to hear
*까치 magpie   혼자 alone
아무도 nobody   저 I/me (polite)

못 AV

An adverb that indicates that a certain action cannot be done or that a certain state has not been achieved. When spoken, 못 is used in front, to be spoken shortly, as in 못 AV, and in writing, it is mainly attached after a verb and used in the form of a long negative sentence, as in AV지 못하다.

(Ex) 전 커피를 **못** 마셔요. I can't drink coffee.

숙제를 다 **못** 했어요. I couldn't do all the homework.

요즘 아침에 잘 **못** 일어납니다. Lately, I can't wake up well in the morning.

그 선수는 이번 시즌에 좋은 기록을 내**지 못**했다.
That player couldn't have a good record this season.

구급차를 받아 주는 병원이 없어서 환자를 살리**지 못**했다.
There were no hospitals that would accept the ambulance, so the patient could not be saved.

1 시에서 강조된 부분의 문법을 분석해 보세요. 어떤 단어와 문법이 쓰였습니까?

Look at the emphasized part of the poem and analyze its grammar. Which words and grammar were used?

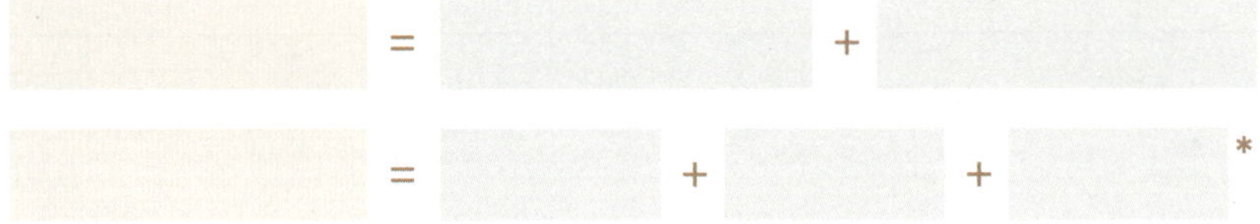

2 다음 표현을 써서 문장을 완성하세요.

Write out the following expressions and complete the sentences.

| 못 | AV지 못하다 |

(가) 저는 테니스를 잘 쳐요. ➡ 저는 테니스를 잘 못 쳐요. 저는 테니스를 잘 치지 못해요.

(나) 매운 음식을 잘 먹어요. ➡ _______________________________

(다) 요즘 밤에 잠을 잘 자요. ➡ _______________________________

(라) 한국어를 그렇게 잘해요. ➡ _______________________________

3 서울 남산에 있는 소나무에서 방금 솔방울 하나가 떨어졌어요. 그 소리를 누가 들었을까요? 왜 그렇게 생각하는지 말해 봅시다.

A pinecone just fell from a pine tree at Namsan in Seoul. Who heard its sound? Explain why you think this.

***-다:** A sentence-closing ending, like -는다, -ㄴ다, -냐, -어라, and -자 used to describe an event, fact, or state of being. They can also be attached after the stem of 이다, an adjective stem, or the endings -으시-, -었-, and -겠-.

A2

(06) 식권

식권은 하루 세끼를 준다.

식모는 젊은 아이들에게
한때 흰 그릇 셋을 준다.

대동강 물로 끓인 국
평안도 쌀로 지은 밥
조선의 매운 고추장

식권은 우리 배를 부르게.

Background Knowledge   In Korean, words that end in -모 (母, meaning "mother") express the meaning of a woman who goes into another person's house and takes care of certain work in order to earn money. For example, a 침모 (針母, meaning "seamstress") who sews clothing, a 찬모 (餐母) who makes side dishes, or a 유모 (乳母, meaning "nanny") who nurses a child instead of its mother, etc., were all jobs that were mainly done by poor women up through the Joseon Dynasty. The word 식모 (食母, meaning "kitchen maid") that appears in this poem has the meaning of a woman who was hired to work in another person's kitchen, a job that existed up through the 1970s. Until the 1980s, most Korean houses and apartments had separate kitchen quarters, and they were provided to kitchen maids as living spaces.

MP3 06

Meal Ticket

The meal ticket provides three meals a day.

The kitchen maid gives to the young children
Three bowls that were once white.

Soup boiled with Daedong River water.
Rice grown in Pyeongan-do.
Joseon's spicy gochujang.

The meal ticket fills our bellies.

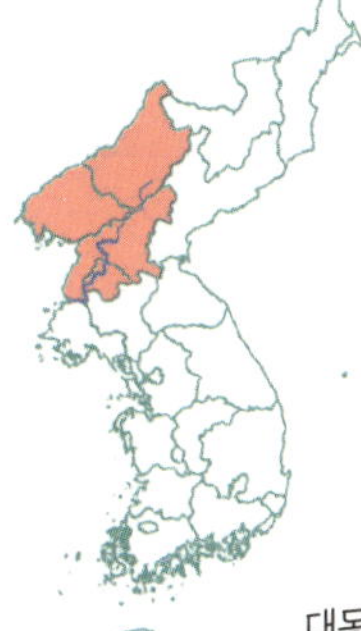

대동강*, 평안도*

Vocabulary _______________

식권 meal ticket	희다 to be white
세끼 three meals	*대동강 Daedong River
식모 kitchen maid	끓이다 to be boiled
젊다 to be young	국 soup
한때 at one time; at once	*평안도 Pyeongan-do Province

N(으)로

A case-marker particle that indicates the material of a certain object. When following a noun without a final consonant, 로 is used. 로 is also used without 으 when following a noun that ends with a final consonant ㄹ.

> **Ex** 사랑은 돈**으로** 살 수 없다. You can't buy love with money.
>
> 오이**로** 얼굴을 마사지해 봤어요? Have you tried massaging your face with cucumber?
>
> 뜨거운 물**로** 샤워를 하니까 기분이 좋아졌어요.
> I took a shower with hot water, so I'm feeling better.
>
> 여러 가지 쌀**로** 지은 밥이 건강에 좋다고 합니다.
> They say that cooking made with various types rice is good for your health.

1 시에서 강조된 부분의 문법을 분석해 보세요. 어떤 단어와 문법이 쓰였습니까?

Look at the emphasized part of the poem and analyze its grammar. Which words and grammar were used?

	=		+	
	=		+	

2 다음 표현을 써서 문장을 완성하세요.

Write out the following expressions and complete the sentences.

N(으)로

(가) 제주 귤   ➡   제주 귤로 만든 초콜릿을 먹어 봤어요? ____________

(나) 이천 쌀   ➡ ____________________________________

(다) 밀양 사과   ➡ ____________________________________

(라) 순창 고추장   ➡ ____________________________________

(마) 강원도 감자   ➡ ____________________________________

(바) 에티오피아 커피   ➡ ____________________________________

3 '햇볕은 쨍쨍'은 1930년부터 지금까지 한국의 아이들이 부르는 노래입니다. 이 노래를 배워서 같이 불러 봅시다.

"햇볕은 쨍쨍" ("The Sun Is Shining") is a song that Korean children have sung from 1930 up through the present. Let's learn the song and sing it together.

햇볕은 쨍쨍

(07) 병아리

"뾰, 뾰, 뾰
　엄마 젖 좀 줘."
　병아리 소리.

"꺽, 꺽, 꺽
　오냐, 좀 기다려."
　엄마 닭 소리.

좀 있다가
병아리들은
엄마 품으로
다 들어갔지요.

Background Knowledge　Yoon Dong-ju began his work seriously in 1936, and at this time, the genre he focused on was children's poetry. Considering that the children's poems *Chicks* and *Broom* were released one after the other in November and December 1936 in a magazine called *Catholic Boys*, which was published at the time in Yanji, it's possible that he focused on creating children's poetry because the literary media in Yanbian at the time was boys' magazines.

MP3 07

Chicks

"Cheep, cheep, cheep!
Mama, feed us."
The sound of chicks.

"Cluck, cluck, cluck!
Wait a moment, darlings."
The sound of mother hen.

After a little while,
The chicks all
Returned to
Their mother's breast.

Vocabulary ____

병아리 chick
젖 milk, breast
오냐 "Okay", "Yes" (an affirmative to someone younger)

닭 chicken
품 breast
들어가다 to go into

An informal sentence-closing ending used when the listener is a similar or younger age than you, or if they are older and are very close with you. This informal form which is mainly used when speaking has the same form for descriptions, questions, demands, and requests.

> (Ex) 같이 **가**. Let's go together.
>
> 밥 먹었**어**? Did you eat?
>
> 10,000원만 좀 빌려**줘**. Lend me just 10,000 won.
>
> 곰 세 마리가 한 집에 있**어**. There are three bears in one house.
>
> 아빠 곰은 뚱뚱**해**. Daddy bear is fat.
>
> 아기 곰은 너무 귀여**워**. Baby bear is very cute.

1 시에서 강조된 부분의 문법을 분석해 보세요. 어떤 단어와 문법이 쓰였습니까?

Look at the emphasized part of the poem and analyze its grammar. Which words and grammar were used?

2 관계있는 것을 연결한 뒤 다음 표현을 써서 문장을 완성하세요.

Connect the items that are related, then write out the following expressions and complete the sentences.

(가) 개	•	• 깍깍 •	• ① 풀을 뜯고 있다.
(나) 소	•	• 야옹 •	• ② 토끼를 따라갔다.
(다) 까치	•	• 짹짹 •	• ③ 책장 위로 올라갔다.
(라) 참새	•	• 멍멍 •	• ④ 한 나무 위로 모였다.
(마) 고양이	•	• 음매 •	• ⑤ 낯선 사람을 보고 짖었다.
(바) 호랑이	•	• 어흥 •	• ⑥ 창문 밖에서 아침 인사를 한다.

(가) 개가 멍멍 하며 낯선 사람을 보고 짖었어.

(나) ____

(다) ____

(라) ____

(마) ____

(바) ____

3 근처 제일 가까운 곳에 있는 동물에게 가서 그 동물이 어떤 소리로 무슨 말을 하는지 들어 봅시다. 여러분의 나라에서는 그 동물의 울음소리를 어떻게 표현하나요?

Go to the closest animal nearby and listen to what sounds it makes and what it's saying. In your home country, how do you express the sound that animal makes?

(08) 가슴 3

불 꺼진 화로를
안고 도는 겨울밤은 깊었다.

재만 남은 가슴이
문풍지 소리에 떤다.

MP3 08

Heart 3

The winter night was deep,
Spent holding and turning around the extinguished brazier.

My heart, left in ashes,
Trembles at the sound of the paper lining the door.

화로*

문풍지*

Vocabulary

가슴 heart, chest, breast
불이 꺼지다 for a flame to go out
*화로 brazier
안고 돌다 to hold and turn
밤이 깊다 for the night to be deep

재가 남다 for ashes to remain
*문풍지 paper weather strip
    (on the door/window)
떨다 to tremble

ㄹ 동사

Refers to verbs with a stem that ends in ㄹ. These irregular ㄹ verbs drop the ㄹ in front of ㅅ, ㄴ, and ㅂ.

> **Ex** 할 일을 다 하고 **노세요**. Do all the work you have to do and then play.
>
> 시험에서 **아는** 문제를 틀렸다. I got a question wrong on the test that I actually knew.
>
> 배가 고파서 눈앞이 빙빙 **돈다**. I'm so hungry that I'm dizzy.

1 시에서 강조된 부분의 문법을 분석해 보세요. 어떤 단어와 문법이 쓰였습니까?
Look at the emphasized part of the poem and analyze its grammar. Which words and grammar were used?

	=		+	
	=		+	

2 다음 표현을 써서 문장을 완성하세요.
Write out the following expressions and complete the sentences.

길다	멀다	알다	살다	만들다

(가) 저는 한국 겨울 날씨를 잘 <u>알니다</u> .

(나) 제가 _________________ 케이크인데 맛이 어때요?

(다) _________________ 머리보다 짧은 머리가 더 편해요.

(라) 저와 누나는 서울에 _________________ 부모님은 부산에 _________________

(마) 제가 사는 원룸은 학교에서 좀 _________________ 방도 크고 값도 싸요.

3 날씨 때문에 잠을 잘 못 잔 적이 있어요? 그런 날 밤에는 어떻게 하면 좋은지 알려 주세요.

Have you ever been unable to sleep because of the weather? Share the best thing to do on nights like that.

Grammar Tip

ㄹ **Irregular Verbs:** Final ㄹ sounds in verb stems disappear before word endings that start with ㄴ, ㅂ, or ㅅ, and before the word ending -오. An example of this is 길다, which becomes 기니, 깁니다, and 기오.

Let's practice how irregular verbs are used.

	-고	-(으)ㄴ/는	-(으)ㄹ	-(스)ㅂ니다
살다				
알다				
팔다				
열다				
놀다				
만들다				
길다				
멀다				

09 할아버지

왜 떡이 쓴데도
자꾸 달다고 하오.

Grandfather

When the rice cake is so bitter,
Why do you always say it's sweet?

Vocabulary

왜 why
떡 rice cake
쓰다 to be bitter

자꾸 repeatedly, again and again
달다 to be sweet

V다고 하오.

In indirect speech, when an elderly person speaks informally but respectfully to someone who isn't that young, they use 하오체(hao-che). Because -오, -소, and -구려 are expressions that were used a lot in the past, you can hear them a lot in dramas set in the past. Depending on whether the information being conveyed is an explanation, question, demand, or request, it can differ between -다고, -냐고, -으라고, and -자고, and be spoken in connection with 하오, which has the same meaning as 합니다 and 해요.

> Ex 벌써 점심을 먹었**냐고 하오**. They're asking if you've already eaten lunch.
>
> 자기들을 기다리지 말**라고 하오**. They said not to wait for them.
>
> 아버님이 지금 댁에 계신**다고 하오**. Father says he's home right now.
>
> 이 음식의 이름은 삼계탕**이라고 하오**. They say this food is called samgyetang.
>
> 아들이 자기하고 같이 한국말을 배우**자고 하오**. My son said I should learn Korean with him.

1 시에서 강조된 부분의 문법을 분석해 보세요. 어떤 단어와 문법이 쓰였습니까?

Look at the emphasized part of the poem and analyze its grammar. Which words and grammar were used?

2 다음 표현을 써서 문장을 완성하세요.

Write out the following expressions and complete the sentences.

-다고	-냐고	-으라고	-자고	N(이)라고

(가) "제게는 그림의 떡입니다."

➡ 자기에게는 그림의 떡이라고 합니다. ______________

(나) "떡 본 김에 제사 지냅시다."

➡ ______________

(다) "이 정도는 누워서 떡 먹기지요."

➡ ______________

(라) "남의 떡이 더 커 보이는 법입니다."

➡ ____

(마) "한국 속담에는 왜 떡이 많이 나와요?"

➡ ____

(바) "떡 줄 사람은 생각도 않는데 김칫국부터 마시지 마세요."

➡ ____

3 한국 사람은 설날에 떡국을 먹고 추석에 송편을 먹습니다. 이사를 하면 시루떡을 만들어서 이웃에게 나눠 주고 아이의 백일에는 백설기를 만들어서 이웃과 나누는 풍습이 있었습니다. 이 떡들에 어떤 의미가 있는지 찾아보세요.

Korean people eat rice cake soup on Lunar New Year and songpyeon (half-moon rice cakes) on Chuseok. When they move to a new house, they make steamed rice cakes and share them with their neighbors, and in the past, there was a custom of making steamed white rice cakes on a baby's 100th day of life to share and eat with neighbors. Find out the meaning that these kinds of rice cakes have.

제사 memorial service, ancestral rites
눕다 to lie down

속담 proverb, saying
김칫국 kimchi(dongchimi) broth

⑩ 호주머니

넣을 것 없어
걱정이던
호주머니는

겨울만 되면
주먹 두 개 갑북갑북.

MP3 10

Pockets

With nothing to hold,
I was worried
About the pockets.

When winter came,
Two fists fill them up, one, two, stuffed full.

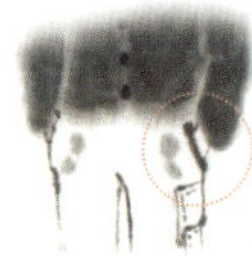
호주머니*

Vocabulary

*호주머니 pocket
걱정이다 to be worried

넣다 to put into
주먹 fist

N만 V(으)면

N만 before -(으)면 indicates the minimum required conditions in order for a certain state to be created. When used with -(으)면, it expresses that the same situation can reoccur whenever those conditions are met.

Ex 숙제**만** 하려고 하**면** 배가 아프다. Whenever I go to do my homework, my stomach hurts.

매년 여름에는 비**만** 오**면** 강물이 넘친다.
Every year in the summer, whenever it rains, the river overflows.

할머니는 나**만** 보**면** 언제나 밥을 먹었냐고 물어보신다.
Whenever my grandmother sees me, she always asks if I've eaten.

1 시에서 강조된 부분의 문법을 분석해 보세요. 어떤 단어와 문법이 쓰였습니까?
Look at the emphasized part of the poem and analyze its grammar. Which words and grammar were used?

     =   +   +

2 다음 표현을 써서 문장을 완성하세요.
Write out the following expressions and complete the sentences.

__________만 __________면 __________다.

(가) 세차를 하다, 비가 오다   ➡ 세차만 하면 비가 온다.

(나) 책을 펴다, 잠이 쏟아지다   ➡ __________

(다) 봄이 되다, 알레르기가 심해지다   ➡ __________

(라) 친구와 약속을 잡다, 회사에 일이 생기다   ➡ __________

(마) 5시 50분이 되다, 퇴근 준비를 하다   ➡ __________

3 지금 주머니 안에 무엇이 있습니까? 만약 주머니 안에 필요한 것이 없다면 어떤 기분이 들지 말해 봅시다.

What is in your pockets right now? If you don't have something you need in your pockets, try describing how that feels.

Rhetoric Tip

Irony: Rhetorical device that emphasizes a meaning that you actually want to convey by expressing the opposite of that meaning. Examples of this are when a child does something wrong and their angry mother says, "Well done!" or when someone sees a lovely child and says, "You look so naughty." In this context, try using the following questions to think about why Yoon Dong-ju emphasizes pockets that are filled only with two fists in the winter.

- What do you think the winter weather was like in 1917-1945, when Yoon Dong-ju lived?
- What did people at that time need during cold winters?
- How would a person whose empty pockets are filled up with just their two fists feel?
- How do you think the poet felt seeing someone who had nothing in their pockets?

Vocabulary

세차 car wash

쏟아지다 to rain, to pour

퇴근 leaving work, getting off work

⑪ 개 1

눈 위에서

개가

꽃을 그리며

뛰오.

Background Knowledge   The fun of this poem is because the phrase 꽃을 그리다 can be interpreted with two meanings. The word 그리다 means "to think of with a longing heart" and "to express the shape of an object in lines or colors, using pencil, etc." The poet, seeing a dog jumping and hopping, leaving footprints that look like flowers on top of the snow, described it as drawing flowers, and at the same time, included wordplay that could be interpreted as the dog running because it misses the flowers.

MP3 11

Dog 1

Atop the snow,
The dog
Draws flowers
As he runs.

Vocabulary

꽃을 그리다 to draw a flower; to long for a flower

Placement of Adverbial Phrases

An adverbial phrase is a phrase made of two or more words that is used like an adverb to describe in detail the meaning of a verb. Like the relationship between 아주 열심히(to the fullest) and 산다(lives) in the sentence 철수는 아주 열심히 산다(Cheolsu lives to the fullest), an adverbial phrase comes right before a predicate (adjective, verb, etc.) – in other words, it is close to the predicate. However, if an adverbial phrase comes at the very start of a sentence, like 눈 위에서(atop the snow) in this poem, it takes on the role of modifying not just the single verb 뛴다(runs) but rather the entire sentence. In this poem, the adverbial phrase indicating the location has four syllables, and a rhythm was created naturally by matching the number of letters in the pattern of "4-2-5-2."

(Ex) **말없이** 떠난 사람 A person who left without a word

조용히 혼자 울어요. They're crying alone quietly.

아쉽게도 시간이 **너무 빨리** 지나요. Unfortunately, time passes too quickly.

1 시에서 강조된 부분의 문법을 분석해 보세요. 어떤 단어와 문법이 쓰였습니까?

Look at the emphasized part of the poem and analyze its grammar. Which words and grammar were used?

2 다음 표현을 써서 문장을 완성하세요.

Write out the following expressions and complete the sentences.

말	배	벌	눈	사과

(가) ___배___ 이/가 아파요.

___배___ 을/를 타고 제주도에 가요.

노랗게 잘 익은 ___배___ 을/를 먹어요.

(나) 빨간 ______________ 이/가 초록색보다 더 맛있어요.

제가 선생님께 잘못을 해서 ______________ 을/를 드리고 싶습니다.

(다) 아침에 _________________을/를 뜨니까 벌써 11시였다.

어제 내린 _________________이/가 거의 녹지 않고 그대로 쌓여 있었다.

(라) _________________이/가 꽃을 찾아다니면서 부지런히 꿀을 만들고 있다.

수업 시간에 떠든 _________________으로/로 화장실 청소를 하게 되었다.

경복궁에 갈 때 한복을 한 _________________ 빌려 입어 보고 싶다.

(마) 발 없는 _________________이/가 천 리를 간다.

바르고 고운 _________________을/를 사용하려고 노력해야 한다.

제주도에 가면 _________________을/를 타 볼 수 있다.

3 누군가를 그리워하는 마음으로 그림을 그린 적이 있어요? 지금 그리운 사람이 있는지 생각해 보고, 그 사람을 생각하면 떠오르는 것들을 그려 보세요.

Have you ever drawn a picture while longing for someone? Think about whether there is someone you miss right now, and draw the things that come to mind when you think of that person.

Vocabulary ____

익다 to ripen
뜨다 to open

리 -ri (a unit of distance, equal to approximately 400 meters)
달리다 to run, to race

(12) 오줌싸개 지도

빨랫줄에 걸어 논
요에다 그린 지도는
지난밤에 내 동생
오줌 싸서 그린 지도

꿈에 가 본 엄마 계신
별나라 지돈가
돈 벌러 간 아빠 계신
만주땅 지돈가

Map of the Bedwetter

Hung on the laundry line,
The map drawn on the floor mattress,
Made last night by my younger sibling,
The map drawn with pee.

Is it a map of the heavens,
Where Mother lives, that he visited in his dreams?
Is it a map of Manchuria,
Where Father went to earn money?

Vocabulary ____

오줌싸개 bedwetter
지도 map
빨랫줄 laundry line
걸다 to hang
놓다 to place
요 floor mattress

오줌 pee
꿈 dream
벌다 to earn
만주 Manchuria
땅 land

N인가, AV는가, DV은가/ㄴ가?

A sentence closing ending that expresses question or surprise about a current fact. In particular, -는가 is attached following the stem of 있다, 없다, or 계시다, or a verb stem, and the word endings -으시-, -었-, or -겠- to make a question about a current situation or fact. It is often used with interrogatives that are frequently used when asking questions, such as 누가, 언제, 어디, 무엇, etc. You can emphasize a meaning of contrast by using opposing information in succession.

(Ex) 그게 정말**인가**? Is that true?

자네 어디 아**픈가**? Are you hurt?

이게 꿈**인가** 생시**인가** 싶다. I wonder if this is a dream or real life.

소문이 꽤 그럴듯해서 **긴가민가**했었다.
The rumor seemed true enough that I was unsure about it.

어느 곳에**선가** 한 번쯤 본 것 같은 얼굴이다.
That seems like a face I've seen before somewhere.

1 시에서 강조된 부분의 문법을 분석해 보세요. 어떤 단어와 문법이 쓰였습니까?
Look at the emphasized part of the poem and analyze its grammar. Which words and grammar were used?

	=		+	

2 다음 표현을 써서 문장을 완성하세요.
Write out the following expressions and complete the sentences.

N인가, AV는가, DV은가/ㄴ가?

(가) 한국어, 쉽다, 어렵다

➡ 한국어는 쉬운가 어려운가?

(나) 명동역, 3호선, 4호선

➡ _______________________________________

(다) 여기(이태원), 한국, 외국

➡ _______________________________________

(라) 커피, 건강에 이롭다, 해롭다

➡ ____

(마) 약속 장소, 고속터미널 역에서 가깝다, 멀다

➡ ____

(바) 한국대학교의 입학식 날짜, 3월 1일, 3월 2일

➡ ____

3 시에서 '별나라'와 '만주땅'은 각각 무엇을 상징할까요? 윤동주가 살았던 시대적 배경을 생각하며 말해 봅시다.

What do "the heavens" and "Manchuria" each symbolize in the poem? Discuss while considering the historical background of the time when Yoon Dong-ju lived.

13 이불

지난밤에
눈이 소 — 복이 왔네
지붕이랑
길이랑 밭이랑
추워한다고
덮어 주는 이불인가 봐

그러기에
추운 겨울에만 내리지

Blanket

Last night,
Snow fell, heaping, heaping.
The roof,
And the road, and the field;
It must have thought they were cold
And covered them up, a blanket.

That's why
Snow only falls in the cold winter.

Vocabulary

소복이 in a heap

지붕 roof

밭 field

덮다 to cover

이불 blanket

N1(이)랑 N2(이)랑 DV어하다

Expresses the meaning that the nouns (N1 and N2) represent a feeling through an object near to them. For example, in this poem, the child thinks that the roof, road, and field seem to be cold in this weather. Attaching -어하다 to an adjective root in this way turns it into a verb. When spoken, it is used with the particles 이랑 and 하고, and in writing, it is mainly used with 와/과, which have the same meaning. These particles are mainly used when connecting two nouns, but can also express the target or level of comparison for the action being described in a sentence.

(Ex) 너**랑** 결혼하고 싶어. I want to marry you.

오늘 친구**랑** 싸웠다. I fought with my friend today.

네가 아버지**랑** 많이 닮았구나. You really resemble your father.

우리 엄마는 아빠**랑** 동갑이다. My mother and father are the same age.

이번 발표는 너**랑** 나**랑** 둘이 하자. Let's you and I do the presentation together this time.

1 시에서 강조된 부분의 문법을 분석해 보세요. 어떤 단어와 문법이 쓰였습니까?

Look at the emphasized part of the poem and analyze its grammar. Which words and grammar were used?

	=		+	
	=		+	
	=		+	

2 다음 표현을 써서 문장을 완성하세요.

Write out the following expressions and complete the sentences.

-네.   N1(이)랑 N2(이)랑 DV어한다고⋯   인가 봐.

(가) 바람이 불다 / 꽃과 나비가 덥다 / 틀어 주는 에어컨

(나) 비가 오다 / 산과 공원이 목마르다 / 뿌려 주는 물

(다) 구름이 끼다 / 새와 나무가 뜨겁다 / 씌워 주는 양산

(라) 달이 밝다 / 너와 내가 밤길이 무섭다 / 켜 주는 가로등

(마) 해가 나다 / 강과 바다가 우울하다 / 위로해 주는 손길

(가) 바람이 부네. 꽃이랑 나비가 더워한다고 틀어 주는 에어컨인가 봐.

(나) ____

(다) ____

(라) ____

(마) ____

3 바람이나 나무 같은 사물에게 감정이 있는 것처럼 느껴진 적이 있어요? 언제 그런 느낌이 들었는지 말해 봅시다.

Have you ever felt as if an object like the wind or a tree has emotions? Describe a time when you felt this way.

Personification: Personification is rhetorical device that expresses inanimate things as if they were animate, or something without emotions as if they were a person with emotions. Examples of this include "the mountains that surround me" or "the weeping sea." In this poem, Yoon Dong-ju described, with the mind of a child, how, upon seeing the snow that had fallen on the roof, road, and field, it was as if someone had thought the world seemed cold and covered it in white snow, like a blanket.

Vocabulary

목마르다 to be thirsty	바르다 to spread, to apply	우울하다 to be depressed
뿌리다 to spray, to sprinkle	가로등 streetlight	위로하다 to comfort

(14) 그 여자

함께 핀 꽃에 처음 익은 능금은
먼저 떨어졌습니다.

오늘도 가을바람은 그냥 붑니다.

길가에 떨어진 붉은 능금은
지나던 손님이 집어 갔습니다.

That Woman

Among the flowers it bloomed alongside, the crab apple
Was the first to fall.

Today as well, the autumn wind simply blows.

The red crab apple, fallen on the roadside;
A person passing by picked it up and went on.

Vocabulary ______________________________

능금 crab apple
떨어지다 to fall
그냥 simply, just
불다 to blow

길가 roadside
붉다 to be red
지나다 to pass by
집다 to pick up

V어/아 (가지고)

-어/아 가지고 expresses that finished result of the action or state that precedes it is maintained, or that the action or state that follows became possible because of the preceding action or state. It is used more in colloquial speech than in writing, and in many cases, 가지고 is shortened to 갖고 or isn't used at all.

(Ex) 그렇게 놀아 갖고 시험에 붙겠니? If you play like that, do you think you'll pass the exam?

날씨가 너무 더워 갖고 공부를 못하겠다. The weather is so hot that I can't study.

은행에 예금된 것을 다 털어 가지고 여행을 다녀왔다.
I emptied out everything I had deposited at the bank and went on a trip.

친구는 명동에서 화장품을 잔뜩 사 가지고 고향에 돌아갔다.
My friend bought a ton of makeup in Myeongdong and brought it back to his hometown.

잠자는 아기의 모습이 너무 귀여워 가지고 눈을 뗄 수가 없었다.
I couldn't take my eyes off the sleeping baby because it was so cute like that.

1 시에서 강조된 부분의 문법을 분석해 보세요. 어떤 단어와 문법이 쓰였습니까?

Look at the emphasized part of the poem and analyze its grammar. Which words and grammar were used?

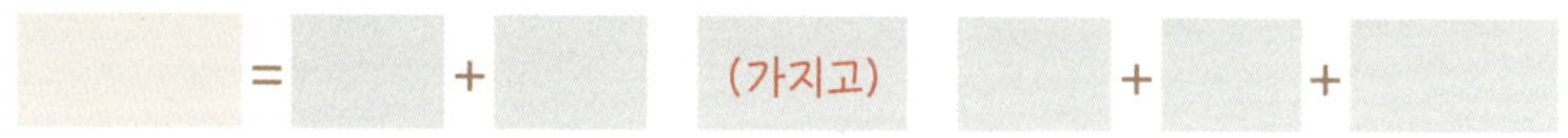

2 다음 표현을 써서 문장을 완성하세요.

Write out the following expressions and complete the sentences.

V어/아 가지고

(가) 사진을 찍다 / 신청서에 붙이세요.

(나) 선물을 하나씩 준비하다 / 오세요.

(다) 시간이 늦다 / 연락을 못 드렸어요.

(라) 점심을 많이 먹다 / 저녁을 못 먹겠다.

(마) 소설을 한 편 쓰다 / 책으로 내고 싶다.

(바) 한국말을 배우다 / 자막 없이 드라마를 보면 좋겠다.

(가) 사진을 찍어 가지고 신청서에 붙이세요.

(나)

(다)

(라)

(마)

(바)

3 이 시의 제목과 내용은 어떤 관계가 있을까요? 사과를 집어 가지고 간 손님은 어떤 사람일지 말해 봅시다.

What is the relationship between the poem's title and its contents? Describe what kind of person picked up and took the apple.

Vocabulary

신청서 application form   자막 subtitles

(15) 해바라기 얼굴

누나의 얼굴은
해바라기 얼굴
해가 금방 뜨자
일터에 간다.

해바라기 얼굴은
누나의 얼굴
얼굴이 숙어 들어
집으로 온다.

MP3 15

Sunflower's Face

My older sister's face
Is a sunflower's face.
As soon as the sun rises,
She goes off to work.

The sunflower's face
Is my older sister's face.
With her face tucked down,
She returns home.

해바라기*

Vocabulary

*해바라기 sunflower
해가 뜨다 for the sun to rise

일터 workplace
숙어 들다 to tuck down

AV자(마자)

A connective ending that expresses that when the preceding action was achieved, the following event or action occurred in succession. It can also be used with 마자 omitted, leaving just -자. However, this weakens the meaning of the following situation occurring immediately after the first. -는 대로, which has a similar meaning to -자(마자), differs in that it is only used when speaking about future plans.

> (Ex) 그는 나를 보**자** 울기 시작했다. When he saw me, he started to cry.
>
> 자동차 세차를 마치**자마자** 비가 쏟아지기 시작했다.
> As soon as I finished getting my car washed, it started pouring rain.
>
> 아침에 일어나**자마자** 휴대 전화 메시지부터 확인한다.
> As soon as I wake up in the morning, I start by checking the messages on my cell phone.
>
> 동생들은 집에 들어서**자마자** 냉장고에서 물부터 꺼내 마셨다.
> As soon as my younger siblings came inside the house, they took out water from the refrigerator and drank it.

1 시에서 강조된 부분의 문법을 분석해 보세요. 어떤 단어와 문법이 쓰였습니까?
Look at the emphasized part of the poem and analyze its grammar. Which words and grammar were used?

	=		+	

2 다음 표현을 써서 문장을 완성하세요.
Write out the following expressions and complete the sentences.

AV자(마자)

(가) 꽃이 피다 / 나비가 모였다.

(나) 우산을 사다 / 비가 그쳤다.

(다) 침대에 눕다 / 잠이 들었다.

(라) 해가 지다 / 기온이 뚝 떨어졌다.

(마) 유튜브 앱을 열다 / 추천 동영상이 떴다.

(가) 꽃이 피자 나비가 모였다.

(나) ________________________________

(다) ________________________________

(라) ________________________________

(마) ________________________________

3 무슨 꽃을 좋아하나요? 그 꽃과 닮은 사람을 떠올려 보세요. 그 사람하고 어떤 추억이 있었는지 말해 봅시다.

What kind of flower do you like? Recall a person who resembles that flower. Describe what kind of memories you have with that person.

Vocabulary ________________________________

나비 butterfly

해가 지다 for the sun to set

기온 temperature

뚝 suddenly

추천 recommendation

동영상 video

떠올리다 to recall

(16) 가슴 2

늗은 가을 쓰르래미
숲에 싸여 공포에 떨고,

웃음 웃는 흰 달 생각이
도망가오.

MP3 16

Heart 2

A cicada shivers of late autumn,
Trembling at the fear surrounded by the forest,

And the thought of the white moon laughing flees.

쓰르래미(쓰르라미)*

Vocabulary ____

*쓰르래미(쓰르라미) cicada
숲 forest
공포 fear

웃다 to laugh
생각 thought
도망가다 to run away, to flee

V(으)ㅁ

An ending that turns a verb into a noun. Like 잠을 자다, 꿈을 꾸다, and 그림을 그리다, 음/ㅁ is attached to a verb stem to make it into a noun. Aside from -(으)ㅁ, the expressions -기 and -는/은/을 것 also turn a verb into a noun. You can often see sentences that end with these nominal forms in lists of things that are done or have to be done, or in writing on message boards that are meant for many people to see. Usually, -음 is used for present or past actions, -기 is used for future plans or decisions, and in "N1 (subject) = N2 (predicate)" sentences with a long subject, the -는/은/을 것 form is used.

> (Ex) 아르바이트 할 사람 구**함**. Looking for someone to do part-time work.
>
> ○월 ○일, 병원에 다녀**옴**. Went to the hospital on MM/DD.
>
> 위 내용은 사실과 틀림없**음**. The above is entirely true.
>
> 우리 식당 음식 재료는 모두 국내산**임**. All ingredients in our restaurant's food are local.
>
> 오늘 야구 경기는 비가 많이 와서 취소**됨**. Today's baseball game canceled due to heavy rain.

1 시에서 강조된 부분의 문법을 분석해 보세요. 어떤 단어와 문법이 쓰였습니까?
Look at the emphasized part of the poem and analyze its grammar. Which words and grammar were used?

2 다음 표현을 써서 문장을 완성하세요.
Write out the following expressions and complete the sentences.

| -(으)ㅁ | -기 | -는/은/을 것 |

(가) 말을 꺼내지 않다 / 만 못하게 됐다.

(나) 유학 생활을 재미있게 즐기다 / 바란다.

(다) 한국어로 팬레터를 쓰다 / 내 꿈이다.

(라) 여행을 가다 / 위해서 한국말을 공부한다.

(마) 밤에 게임을 안 하기로 마음먹다 / 쉽지 않다.

(바) 요즘 할 일이 많다 / 때문에 시간을 내기가 좀 어렵다.

(가)

(나)

(다)

(라)

(마)

(바)

3 늦가을 숲속에서 쓰르라미를 보게 된다면 어떤 느낌이 들것 같아요? 그 숲에서 19살 윤동주 시인을 만난다면 어떤 말을 해 주고 싶은지 생각해 봅시다.

How do you think you would feel if you saw a cicada in the forest in the late autumn? Think about what you would like to say to the 19-year-old poet Yoon Dong-ju if you met him in that forest.

(17) 반딧불

가자, 가자, 가자,
숲으로 가자.
달 조각을 주우러
숲으로 가자.

그믐밤 반딧불은
부서진 달 조각

가자, 가자, 가자,
숲으로 가자.
달 조각을 주우러
숲으로 가자.

Background Knowledge   When he wrote this poem in 1937, Yoon Dong-ju was a basketball player at Gwangmyeong Middle School. That year, he came into conflict with his father over his career path. His father strongly wished for him to go to medical or law school, but he insisted on going to a liberal arts school. It's said that he clashed with his father over this issue every day, to the degree that dishes and cups were thrown around the house. His grandfather, who cherished him, took his side, and in 1938, he was able to enter the liberal arts school at Yonhi College(Chosen Christian College) (known today as Yonsei University). In his essay *Shoot the Moon*, which was submitted to the *Chosun Daily* in October 1938 and published January 1939, there is a scene in which he sees the moon reflected in a pond at Yonsei University on an autumn night, and makes a slingshot out of a tree branch and shoots the moon. Around the age of 20 Yoon Dong-ju seems to have been so interested in the moon, moonlight, and shadows from the moon that he saw autumn fireflies and thought of them as shards of the moon.

MP3 17

Fireflies

Let's go, let's go, let's go,
Let's go into the woods.
To gather up shards of the moon,
Let's go into the woods.

On the last night of the month, the fireflies
Are shards of the shattered moon.

Let's go, let's go, let's go,
Let's go into the woods.
To gather up shards of the moon,
Let's go into the woods.

반딧불*

Vocabulary

*반딧불 firefly
조각 piece, shard
그믐밤 the last night of a lunar month

부서지다 to shatter, to break
줍다 to gather

AV(으)러 N(으)로 가자

-(으)러 is a connective ending that expresses the purpose of an action or of going to a certain place, and -자 is an informal sentence-closing ending that expresses the meaning of requesting to do a certain action together. N에 can be used when placing special emphasis on the place where the requested action will take place, but is narrow and indicates only that specific place, whereas using N으로 has the meaning of widely indicating the area where that place is located.

> *Ex* 친구를 만나**러** 홍대 앞에 **간다**. I'm going to Hongdae to meet a friend.
>
> 점심시간인데 밥 먹**으러 나가자**. It's lunchtime; let's go out to eat.
>
> 지난번에 네게 맡긴 가방을 찾**으러 왔어**. I came to get the bag I left with you last time.
>
> 철수 씨, 오늘 우리 부모님을 뵈**러** 집에 같이 **가요**.
> Mr. Cheolsu, let's go to my house with me today to see my parents.

1 시에서 강조된 부분의 문법을 분석해 보세요. 어떤 단어와 문법이 쓰였습니까?

Look at the emphasized part of the poem and analyze its grammar. Which words and grammar were used?

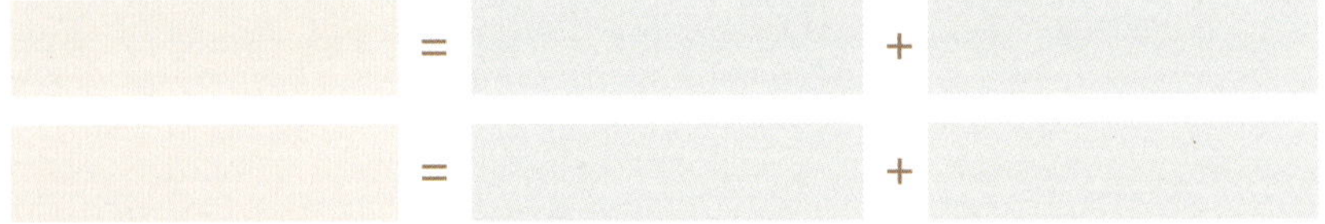

2 다음 표현을 써서 문장을 완성하세요.

Write out the following expressions and complete the sentences.

AV(으)러 N(으)로 가자/나가자.

(가) 일출을 보다 / 동해

(나) 시험 공부를 하다 / 카페

(다) 눈사람을 만들다 / 운동장

(라) 벚꽃 사진을 찍다 / 여의도

(마) 단풍 구경을 하다 / 설악산

(가) <u>일출을 보러 동해로 가자.</u>

(나) ____

(다) ____

(라) ____

(마) ____

3 <나는 반딧불>이라는 노래를 찾아서 듣고 가사의 의미를 알아봅시다. 그리고 그 의미를
윤동주의 <반딧불>과 비교해 봅시다.

Look up the song "나는 반딧불(I'm a Firefly)" and listen to it, and find out the meaning of
the lyrics. Then, compare that meaning to Yoon Dong-ju's "Fireflies."

Vocabulary

일출 sunrise

동해 East Sea

눈사람 snowman

벚꽃 cherry blossoms

여의도 Yeouido

단풍 autumn foliage

설악산 Mount Seoraksan

(18) 산협의 오후

내 노래는 오히려
서러운 산울림.

골짜기 길에
떨어진 그림자는
너무나 슬프구나.

오후의 명상은
아 —— 졸려.

Mountain Valley Afternoon

My song is, in fact,
A sorrowful mountain echo.

On the valley road,
My shadow, fallen
Is so very sad.

This afternoon's contemplation:
Oh – I am sleepy.

산협 mountain valley

서럽다 to be sorrowful

골짜기 valley

그림자 shadow

명상 meditation, contemplation

졸리다 to be sleepy, to be tired

Used to convey wonder about something to a younger listener or to yourself. There are generally two types of casual speech used with someone younger than yourself: formal and informal. Formal casual speech such as AV는다, DV다, and N이다 is mainly used in official declarative statements; otherwise, V니?, AV어라, AV자, AV는구나, DV구나, and other formal casual questions, demands, and requests that express wonder are used when there is a large age difference, only by a superior to a subordinate or when the relationship between two people is very close. Informal casual speech in the form of V어/아/여. is often used between two people of the same age.

(Ex) 같이 가**자**. Let's go together.

밥 먹었**니**? Have you eaten?

어서 들어가 자**라**. Hurry home and sleep.

너는 한국 친구가 정말 많**구나**. Wow, you really have a lot of Korean friends.

한국에는 봄, 여름, 가을, 겨울, 사계절이 **있다**.
Korea has four distinct seasons: spring, summer, fall, and winter.

1 시에서 강조된 부분의 문법을 분석해 보세요. 어떤 단어와 문법이 쓰였습니까?

Look at the emphasized part of the poem and analyze its grammar. Which words and grammar were used?

2 다음 표현을 써서 문장을 완성하세요.

Write out the following expressions and complete the sentences.

DV다., AV는다., N이다., V니?, AV어/아라., AV자., AV는구나., DV구나.

(가) 윤동주가 남긴 시는 모두 119편입니다.

(나) 윤동주가 사용한 시어는 참 아름답습니다.

(다) 윤동주의 다른 시들도 검색해 보세요.

(라) '산협'과 같은 뜻을 가진 단어를 찾아봅시다.

(마) 한글 시를 이해하려면 한자도 좀 알아야 되는군요.

(바) 이 시 말고 다른 한글 시를 읽어 본 적이 있습니까?

(가) 윤동주가 남긴 시는 모두 119편이다.

(나)

(다)

(라)

(마)

(바)

3 명상을 해 본 적이 있어요? 언제 명상을 하고 싶어지는지 말해 봅시다.
Have you ever tried meditating? Discuss the times when you feel like meditating.

Vocabulary

검색하다 to search   시어 poetic diction

19 고향집
－만주에서 부른

헌 짚신짝 끄을고
나 여기 왜 왔나
두만강을 건너서
쓸쓸한 이 땅에

남쪽 하늘 저 밑엔
따뜻한 내 고향
내 어머니 계신 곳
그리운 고향집.

Background Knowledge

In this poem, written in 1936, Yoon Dong-ju is in missing his hometown in the south of the Korean Peninsula, across the Tumen River from Manchuria. In other words, his nationality is that of the country on the Korean Peninsula.

MP3 19

My Home in My Hometown
—Called for from Manchuria

Dragging, dragging my old straw shoes,
Why have I come here?
Across the Tumen River
To this lonesome land.

Under the southern sky
Is my warm hometown.
The place where my mother is.
The home that I long for.

짚신짝*

Vocabulary

고향 hometown	쓸쓸하다 to be lonesome
부르다 to call	남쪽 south, southern
헐다 to be old, to be worn out	밑 under
*짚신짝 a single straw shoe	계시다 to be (polite)
끌다 to drag	그립다 to long for, to miss

AV고, AV어/아서

If the order of the preceding and following actions cannot be changed, they are connected with -어서. However, for verbs where a person's body is directly touched, such as "어깨에 가방을 메다(to put a bag over one's shoulders)", "운동화 끈을 매다(to tie one's shoelaces)", and "슬리퍼를 끌다 (to drag one's slippers)" – in other words, "body-attached verbs" – order must be indicated by attaching -고 to the verb stem and connecting it to a different action that follows. Otherwise, -고 is usually used when connecting actions whose order can be reversed, such as in "먼저 숙제하고 그 후에 놀자 (Let's do our homework first and then play)." and "먼저 놀고 나서 그 다음에 숙제 할 것이다(I'll play first and then afterwards, I'll do my homework)."

(Ex) 날마다 버스를 타고 학교에 간다. Every day, I take the bus to go to school.

이 물건은 바다를 건너서 온 수입품이다.
This item is an imported product that came after crossing the ocean.

친구가 나를 보고 횡단보도를 건너서 뛰어왔다.
My friend saw me and ran across the crosswalk to me.

오늘은 날씨가 추워서 코트를 입고 장갑까지 끼고 나갔다.
Since the weather was cold today, I wore a coat and gloves when I went out.

---

1 시에서 강조된 부분의 문법을 분석해 보세요. 어떤 단어와 문법이 쓰였습니까?

Look at the emphasized part of the poem and analyze its grammar. Which words and grammar were used?

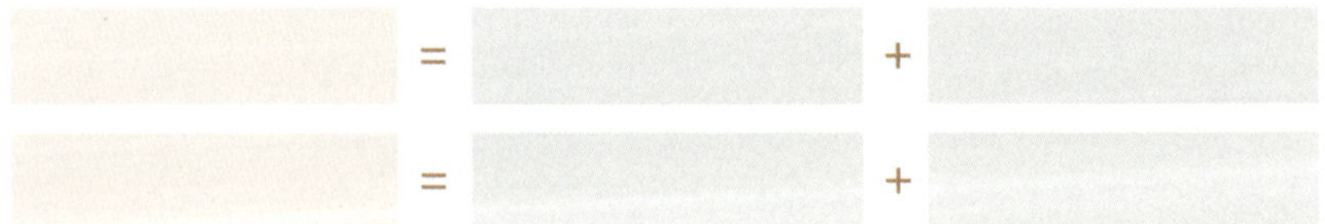

	=		+	
	=		+	

2 다음 표현을 써서 문장을 완성하세요.

Write out the following expressions and complete the sentences.

AV고   AV어/아서

(가) 옷을 따뜻하게 입다 / 학교에 가라.

(나) 카페에 들르다 / 커피를 사 가지고 수업에 간다.

(다) 오늘 아침에 일어나다 / 뉴스부터 확인했다.

(라) 한복을 입다 / 경복궁에 가면 무료로 입장할 수 있다.

(마) 친구를 만나다 / 같이 고속버스 터미널에 가려고 한다.

(바) 감기가 유행할 때는 마스크를 끼다 / 버스를 타는 게 좋다.

(가) 옷을 따뜻하게 입고 학교에 가라. ______________________________

(나) ______________________________

(다) ______________________________

(라) ______________________________

(마) ______________________________

(바) ______________________________

3 고향에 지금 누가 살고 있어요? 고향집을 생각하면 어떤 기분이 드는지 말해 봅시다.
Who is living in your hometown right now? Discuss how it feels when you think of your house back home.

Vocabulary ____

간밤 last night

(20) 새로운 길

내를 건너서 숲으로
고개를 넘어서 마을로

어제도 가고 오늘도 갈
나의 길 새로운 길

민들레가 피고 까치가 날고
아가씨가 지나고 바람이 일고

나의 길은 언제나 새로운 길
오늘도 …… 내일도 ……

내를 건너서 숲으로
고개를 넘어서 마을로

Background Knowledge

In February 1938, three months before this poem was created, Yoon Dong-ju graduated from the fifth grade of Gwangmyeong Middle School, and in April, he entered the liberal arts school at Yonhi College(Chosen Christian College), where he lived in a dormitory for three years. He learned from Professors Choi Hyeon-bae and Lee Yang-ha, and during summer vacation in 1938, taught at a summer bible school at Northern Church in Yongjeong. Today, on the Sinchon Campus of Yonsei University in Seoul, there is a pine forest called Cheongsongdae Park. The campus's main building, which was used for the school of liberal arts until 1980, is located near this forest. Perhaps Yoon Dong-ju would come out of his dormitory (today's Yoon Dong-ju Memorial Hall), study at the school of liberal arts (today's main building), and look at the natural environment of Cheongsongdae Park while making decisions about "a new path" for his life.

MP3 20

A New Path

Across the stream and into the woods,
Over the hill and toward the village,

It went yesterday and will go today as well.
My path, my new path.

Dandelions bloom, and magpies fly,
And a young lady passes by, and the wind rises,

My path is always a new path.
Today······ and tomorrow······

Across the stream and into the woods,
Over the hill and toward the village.

내 stream		민들레 dandelion
숲 woods, forest		아가씨 young lady
고개 hill		일다 to rise
마을 village		

N(으)로

A case-marker particle that expresses the direction in which the subject moves toward a target. Following verbs that end with a final consonant ㄹ or a vowel, 로 is used. (으)로 is also used to express a tool or material.

(Ex) 약속 장소**로** 가는 길이다. I'm on my way to the meeting place.

한국에서는 수저**로** 음식을 먹는다. In Korea, people eat with spoon and chopsticks.

아이가 놓친 풍선이 하늘**로** 올라갔다. The balloon that the child let go of rose into the sky.

된장과 두부는 콩**으로** 만든 음식이다. Soybean paste and tofu are foods made with beans.

그는 미국**으로** 한 달 동안 여행을 떠났다. He left for America on a month-long trip.

1 시에서 강조된 부분의 문법을 분석해 보세요. 어떤 단어와 문법이 쓰였습니까?

Look at the emphasized part of the poem and analyze its grammar. Which words and grammar were used?

	=		+	
	=		+	

2 다음 표현을 써서 문장을 완성하세요.

Write out the following expressions and complete the sentences.

N(으)로

(가) 끝 / 가서 줄을 서세요.

(나) 어디 / 가야 할지 모르겠다.

(다) 기사님, 서울역 / 가 주세요.

(라) 하늘 / 솟았나, 땅속 / 꺼졌나.

(마) 오른쪽 / 쭉 가시면 공원이 나올 거예요.

(바) 꼭대기 층 / 올라가시면 전망이 더 좋습니다.

(가) 끝으로 가서 줄을 서세요.

(나) ____

(다) ____

(라) ____

(마) ____

(바) ____

3 여러분이 날마다 다니는 길은 어떤 길인지, 그 길에서는 무엇이 보이는지 말해 봅시다.
Discuss what paths you walk along each day and what you see along those paths.

하늘로 솟다 to rise into the sky 　　　　땅으로 꺼지다 to fall to the ground, to break down
꼭대기 top, apex 　　　　전망 view

㉑ 귀뚜라미와 나와

귀뚜라미와 나와
잔디밭에서 이야기했다.

귀뜰귀뜰
귀뜰귀뜰

아무에게도 알려 주지 말고
우리들만 알자고 약속했다.

귀뜰귀뜰
귀뜰귀뜰

귀뚜라미와 나와
달 밝은 밤에 이야기했다.

MP3 21

The cricket and I

The cricket and I
Spoke out on the grass.

Chirp, chirp!
Chirp, chirp!

We promised not to tell anyone,
Said only the two of us would know.

Chirp, chirp!
Chirp, chirp!

The cricket and I
Spoke in the night made bright with the moon.

Vocabulary ——————————————————————————————

귀뚜라미 cricket
잔디밭 grass

알리다 to tell, to inform

An expression preventing the action(AV1) in the preceding clause and advising the different action(AV2) in the following clause. When advising that a positive new action be done instead of a negative action, AV1지 말고 AV2어라 is used, and when the speaker wishes that the action be done with them, AV1지 말고 AV2자 is used. When advising the listener gently or when talking to yourself, an expression that indicates a decision, like AV어야지 or AV어야겠다, is added.

(Ex) 비가 그치기를 기다리**지 말고** 우산을 사자.
Let's not wait for the rain to stop and buy an umbrella.

패스트푸드만 먹**지 말고** 직접 요리도 좀 해야겠다.
I need to not just eat fast food and cook and eat for myself instead.

내일부터는 밤에 동영상을 보**지 말고** 일찍 자야지.
Starting tomorrow, I need to not watch videos and go to sleep early instead.

이번 여름에는 해외여행을 가**지 말고** 국내 여행을 가자.
Let's go on a domestic trip instead of traveling abroad this summer.

1 시에서 강조된 부분의 문법을 분석해 보세요. 어떤 단어와 문법이 쓰였습니까?
Look at the emphasized part of the poem and analyze its grammar. Which words and grammar were used?

2 두 가지를 비교하여 더 좋은 방법을 제안하는 문장을 완성하세요.
Compare the two items and create a sentence that suggests a better method.

AV1지 말고 AV2자.

(가) 잘하는 일만 하다   •

(나) 가능하면 밥은 혼자 먹다   •

(다) 여행은 다리가 떨릴 때 가다   •

• ① 가슴이 떨릴 때 가다

• ② 좋아하는 사람과 먹다

• ③ 바로 지금 연락해 보다

(라) 돈을 많이 벌려고만 하다　　•　　　　　•　④ 가끔은 좋아하는 일도 하다

(마) 부모님을 생각만 하다　　•　　　　　•　⑤ 잘 쓰는 방법을 생각해 보다

(가) 잘하는 일만 하지 말고 가끔은 좋아하는 일도 하자.

(나) ____

(다) ____

(라) ____

(마) ____

3 "AV1지 말고 AV2자고 마음먹었었다." 라는 표현을 써서 새해 또는 새 학기를 맞이할 때 지난해 또는 지난 학기에 대해 어떤 반성과 결심을 했는지 말해 봅시다.

Using the expression "AV1지 말고 AV2자고 마음먹었었다," discuss what reflections or decisions you made last year or last semester about the new year or new semester.

Vocabulary ____

결심 decision

㉒ 바람이 불어

바람이 어디로부터 불어와
어디로 불려 가는 것일까.

바람이 부는데
내 괴로움에는 이유가 없다.

내 괴로움에는 이유가 없을까.

단 한 여자를 사랑한 일도 없다.
시대를 슬퍼한 일도 없다.

바람이 자꾸 부는데
내 발이 반석 위에 섰다.

강물이 자꾸 흐르는데
내 발이 언덕 위에 섰다.

MP3 22

The Wind Blows

Where does the wind blow in from,
And where does it blow out to?

The wind blows,
And there is no reason for my suffering.

Is there no reason for my suffering?

Never have I loved a woman,
And never have I lamented the age.

The wind blows on and on,
And I am stood with my feet upon a rock.

The river flows on and on,
And I am stood with my feet upon a hill.

Vocabulary ____

불려 가다 to blow out   반석 rock
괴로움 suffering, torment   강물 river, river water
이유 reason   언덕 hill
시대 age, period, era

AV는데/DV은데/N인데

A connective ending used when revealing the background of a situation in the clause that follows, or when presenting in advance a situation in the preceding clause that is related to the clause that follows, in order to explain information that contrasts with the situation in the clause that follows.

> (Ex) 눈이 오**는데** 운전을 해도 될까? It's snowing; is it alright to drive?
>
> 그 가수는 노래는 잘 부르**는데** 춤은 잘 못 춰.
> That singer sings well, but doesn't dance well.
>
> 퇴근 시간이 다 됐**는데** 회의가 아직 안 끝났다.
> It's time to clock out, but the meeting is not over yet.
>
> 시를 고치고 있**는데** 어떻게 고치면 좋을지 생각이 잘 안 난다.
> I'm fixing up my poem, but I can't think of a good way to do it.

1 시에서 강조된 부분의 문법을 분석해 보세요. 어떤 단어와 문법이 쓰였습니까?
Look at the emphasized part of the poem and analyze its grammar. Which words and grammar were used?

2 다음 표현을 써서 문장을 완성하세요.
Write out the following expressions and complete the sentences.

AV는데, DV은데, N인데

(가) K-Pop이 좋다 / 가사를 잘 모르겠다.

(나) 남산한옥마을에 가고 싶다 / 길을 모른다.

(다) 지금 몇 시 / 아직까지 점심을 안 먹었니?

(라) 한국 음식을 좋아하다 / 매운 건 못 먹는다.

(마) 요즘 한국 드라마를 보다 / 자막이 없으면 안 된다.

(바) 한복을 처음 입어 봤다 / 생각보다 가볍고 편했다.

(가) K-Pop이 좋은데 가사를 잘 모르겠다. ___________________________

(나) ____

(다) ____

(라) ____

(마) ____

(바) ____

3 바람이 세게 부는 날에 강물이 흐르고 있다면 어떤 모습일까요? 만약 여러분이 그 모습을 본다면 어떤 기분이 들까요?
What would it look like if a river was flowing on a very windy day? How would you feel if you saw that?

Vocabulary ____

가사 lyrics
남산한옥마을 Namsan Hanok Village (a neighborhood in Seoul with many hanok houses)

(23) 비 뒤

"어 — 얼마나 반가운 비냐"
할아버지의 즐거움.

가물 들었던 곡식 자라는 소리
할아버지 담배 빠는 소리와 같다.

비 뒤의 햇살은
풀잎에 아름답기도 하다.

Background Knowledge

As a young man, Yoon Dong-ju was influenced in many ways by a poem by poet Jeong Ji-yong (1902-1950). Both poems by Yoon Dong-ju and Jeong Ji-yong have in common that they were written from the point of view of a child watching their grandfather farm. Like in that other poem, the subject matter of a grandfather, cigarettes, and rain also appear in the poem *Grandfather*. However, they are different in that the child in Jeong Ji-yong's poem is simply surprised at how his grandfather always seems to know the day's weather and dress for it correctly. But the child in Yoon Dong-ju's poem *Grandfather* happily greets the first rain in a long time with his grandfather, thinking of it as beautiful, and the strong tenacity of the grain is conveyed through a clear, auditory image.

After the Rain

"Oh — What a welcome rain!"
Grandfather's joy.

The sound of the grain growing after having fallen into drought
Is like the sound of Grandfather sucking on his tobacco pipe.

And the sunlight after the rain
Is lovely on the blades of grass, as well.

Vocabulary ______________________________________

가물(가뭄) drought	빨다 to suck
곡식 grain	햇살 sunshine
자라다 to grow	풀잎 blade of grass
담배 tobacco, cigarette	

(N1은/는) 얼마나 DV(으)ㄴ N2(이)냐

An expression that emphasizes the state or degree of the subject, used with the adverb 얼마나, indicating the degree of a state is very large, and the interrogative sentence-closing ending -냐. N2 is a word that indicates the category to which N1 belongs, and to emphasize surprise about the omitted subject N1, the order is changed to DV(으)ㄴ N2. 이 can also be used in place of the omitted N1. For example, to emphasize that "한국어가 아주 어렵다(Korean is very difficult).", the sentence can be changed and expressed as "(한국어는) 이 얼마나 어려운 언어인가(What a difficult language this (Korean) is)." When using the interrogative sentence-closing ending -니 instead of -냐, it emphasizes the feeling of looking for agreement, and when using -는가, it emphasizes the meaning of surprise.

> (Ex) **얼마나** 놀라운 선물**인가**. What a surprising gift.
>
> **얼마나** 시원한 바람**이냐**. What a refreshing breeze.
>
> **얼마나** 반가운 소식**이니**. What welcome news.
>
> 이 **얼마나** 신나는 말**인가**. What an exciting thing to say.
>
> **얼마나** 아름다운 풍경**이냐**. What beautiful scenery.

1 시에서 강조된 부분의 문법을 분석해 보세요. 어떤 단어와 문법이 쓰였습니까?

Look at the emphasized part of the poem and analyze its grammar. Which words and grammar were used?

2 다음 표현을 써서 문장을 완성하세요.

Write out the following expressions and complete the sentences.

이 얼마나 DV(으)ㄴ N(이)냐

(가) 아이가 너무 귀엽게 웃는다.

(나) 이 가게 김치찌개 맛이 예술이다.

(다) 가을 하늘이 구름 한 점 없이 맑다.

(라) 소설가 한강의 작품이 매우 감동적이다.

(마) 피아노 연주 소리가 아주 아름답다.

(바) 딸의 졸업식을 보니 정말 행복하다.

(가) 이 얼마나 귀여운 아이냐.

(나) ____

(다) ____

(라) ____

(마) ____

(바) ____

3 할아버지께서 비를 반가워하신 이유에 대해서 생각해 봅시다.
Think about the reason why the grandfather might be pleased to see the rain.

B1

24 사과

붉은 사과 한 개를
아버지 어머니
누나, 나, 넷이서
껍질째로 속까지
다 — 나눠 먹었소.

MP3 24

Apple

One red apple,
For Father, Mother,
Older Sister, and I, split in four,
Unpeeled, right through to the core,
We shared and ate it all – up.

Vocabulary

껍질 peel, skin

째 whole

속 Inside, core

나누다 to share

N이서

A case-marker particle that is attached to a noun expressing a number (like혼자(alone), 둘(two), 셋(three), 넷(four)) to express that that word is the subject. Only used when the noun expresses a number of people, and is mainly used only in spoken situations and not in writing.

Ex 아이가 혼자**서** 집을 지키고 있었다. The child was watching the house alone.

아이 둘과 나, 이렇게 셋**이서** 여행을 갔다.
The three of us went on a trip, the two children and I.

둘이서 싸우지 말고 사이좋게 나눠 먹어라.
Don't fight between the two of you and eat it together nicely.

이번 학기에는 친구 셋이랑 나까지 모두 넷**이서** 아파트를 얻어 지내기로 했다.
This semester, I and three of my friends decided to get an apartment and live together, the four of us.

---

1 시에서 강조된 부분의 문법을 분석해 보세요. 어떤 단어와 문법이 쓰였습니까?
Look at the emphasized part of the poem and analyze its grammar. Which words and grammar were used?

	=		+	

2 다음 표현을 써서 문장을 완성하세요.
Write out the following expressions and complete the sentences.

N이서

(가) 둘 / 피자 한 판이면 될까?

(나) 셋 / 할 수 있는 보드게임을 알아?

(다) 넷 / 택시 한 대로 갈 수 있겠지?

(라) 다섯 / 이만 원씩 모으면 십만 원이 되겠다.

(마) 아홉 / 한데 다 묵으려면 펜션을 예약해야겠다.

(가) **둘이서 피자 한 판이면 될까?**

(나) ____

(다) ____

(라) ____

(마) ____

3 사과 한 개를 최대 몇 명까지 나눠 먹어 봤어요? 왜 그렇게 나눠 먹었는지 말해 봅시다.

How many people have you shared a single apple with before? Discuss why you shared the apple like that.

Vocabulary

한 판 one pie
한 대 one car
한데 one place
묵다 to stay

펜션 pension
예약하다 to reserve
최대 maximum, at most

(25) 슬픈 족속

흰 수건이 검은 머리를 두르고
흰 고무신이 거친 발에 걸리우다.

흰 저고리 치마가 슬픈 몸집을 가리고
흰 띠가 가는 허리를 질끈 동이다.

Background Knowledge

As in the sentence "시인이 (animate being + subject marker) 시를 (inanimate being + object marker) 쓴다 (verb)" ("The poet writes a poem."), it is natural in Korean sentences for a character that can feel emotions to be in the place of the subject. The reason that "아이가 만두를 먹는다(A child eats a dumpling)." is a better sentence than "만두가 아이에게 먹힌다(A dumpling is eaten by a child)." is because a child, who can feel emotions, is better suited to the place of the subject than a dumpling. However, in poetry, breaking these rules of grammar can provide a fresh feeling, rhetorically.

A Sorry People

White cloth wrapped around black hair,
White rubber shoes caught on coarse feet.

White jeogori and skirts hiding sorry frames,
White bands clinching slender waists tight.

Vocabulary

족속 a people, a race	몸집 frame, build (of a body)
수건 cloth	띠 band, sash, belt
검다 to be black	가늘다 to be thin
고무신 rubber shoes	허리 waist
거칠다 to be coarse, to be rough	질끈 clench tight
저고리 jeogori (the upper part of a hanbok)	동이다 to tie
치마 skirt	

-는/은/ㄴ/을/ㄹ N

An adnominal form ending, attached after a verb or adjective, that modifies a noun. It is used differently depending on tense and whether or not the stem has a final consonant. With the past tense of a verb's adnominal form, -은/ㄴ is used; with the present tense adnominal form, -는 is used; and with the future adnominal form, -을/ㄹ is used. With an adjective's adnominal form, -은/ㄴ is used. When the verb or adjective stem ends with a vowel, only ㄴ or ㄹ is used, without 으.

Ex 친구가 **좋은** 영화를 추천해 줬다. My friend recommended me a good movie.

지금 네가 **보는** 영상은 누가 만든 거니? Who made the video you're watching now?

고향에서 **보낸** 소포를 사흘 만에 받았다.
I've received a package sent from my hometown in only three days.

일정표에서 다음 주에 **할** 일을 확인해 봐라.
Check the schedule for the work you have to do next week.

1 시에서 강조된 부분의 문법을 분석해 보세요. 어떤 단어와 문법이 쓰였습니까?

Look at the emphasized part of the poem and analyze its grammar. Which words and grammar were used?

	=		+	
	=		+	
	=		+	
	=		+	
	=		+	

2 다음 밑줄 친 표현의 의미를 [보기]에서 찾아 쓰십시오.
Find the meaning of the following underlined expressions in the word bank and write them out.

[보기]	도둑	음식	간호사	한민족	식사 대접

(가) 사람이 <u>빵</u>만으로 사는 것은 아니다.

    음식

(나) 휴가철에 집을 비울 때는 <u>밤손님</u>을 조심해야 한다.

(다) 장학금을 받았다고? 네 공부 도와준 나한테 <u>한턱낼</u> 거지?

(라) 응급 상황에서 환자를 살린 <u>백의의 천사</u>가 한둘이 아니다.

(마) 한국 사람이 흰옷을 즐겨 입었던 데에서 <u>백의민족</u>이라는 표현이 유래됐다.

3 한국을 생각하면 어떤 색깔이 떠오르는지, 왜 그 색깔을 골랐는지 말해 봅시다.
Discuss what color comes to mind when you think of Korea, and why you chose that color.

Vocabulary

대접 treatment	천사 angel
휴가철 holiday(vacation) season	즐겨 입다 to enjoy wearing
조심하다 to be careful	백의민족 the people in white (a term for the Korean people)
장학금 scholarship	표현 expression
한턱내다 to treat (someone to something)	유래 origin
응급 상황 emergency situation	색깔 color
백의 white clothing	고르다 to choose

26 서시

죽는 날까지 하늘을 우러러
한점 부끄럼이 없기를,
잎새에 이는 바람에도
나는 괴로워했다.
별을 노래하는 마음으로
모든 죽어가는 것을 사랑해야지
그리고 나한테 주어진 길을
걸어가야겠다.

오늘밤에도 별이 바람에 스치운다.

Background Knowledge

The title of this poem is known as *Prologue*, but it actually came to be called *Prologue* because it was the work placed first out of the 19 poems chosen and collected by Yoon Dong-ju himself.

MP3 26

Prologue

Until the day I die,
As I look up toward the heavens,
Wishing not to have a speck of shame,
I have suffered even at the wind that stirs the leaves.
With a heart singing the stars,
I must love all things that are dying,
And I must walk along
The path that was given to me.

Tonight, again, the stars are blown by the wind.

Vocabulary

서시 prologue
죽다 to die
우러르다 to respect, to raise one's head
부끄럼 shame
잎새 leaf
괴로워하다 to suffer

별 star
모든 all, every
주어지다 to be given
걸어가다 to walk down
스치다 to brush, to graze

AV어/아야지.

A sentence closing ending that expresses a meaning of seeking agreement about a duty that the listener must perform. It also expresses the speaker's will when talking to themself. Like in the sentences "나도 가지(I'm going, too)." or "늦었는데 이제 그만 일어나지(It's late; We should get up now).", this sentence-final ending is attached after endings like -으시-, -았-, and -겠-, and expresses the meaning of positively describing, asking, ordering, or recommending something.

> (Ex) 발목을 삐었으면 많이 걷지 말**아야지**.
> If you've sprained your ankle, you shouldn't walk much.
>
> 오늘 집에 못 들어올 것 같으면 연락을 했**어야지**.
> If you thought you wouldn't be able to come home today, you should have contacted me.

1 시에서 강조된 부분의 문법을 분석해 보세요. 어떤 단어와 문법이 쓰였습니까?
Look at the emphasized part of the poem and analyze its grammar. Which words and grammar were used?

<table>
<tr><td> </td><td>=</td><td> </td><td>+</td><td> </td><td>+</td><td> </td></tr>
</table>

2 다음 표현을 써서 문장을 완성하세요.
Write out the following expressions and complete the sentences.

AV어/아야지.

(가) 교실에서는 한글 이름을 쓰다

(나) 내 한글 이름을 예쁘게 짓다

(다) 예쁜 이름을 몇 개 선생님께 묻다

(라) 친구를 부를 때 한글 이름으로 부르다

(마) 내 이름을 짓고 나서 친구가 이름 짓는 걸 돕다

(가) 교실에서는 한글 이름을 써야지.

(나) ____

(다) ____

(라) ____

(마) ____

3 여러분은 요즘 바라는 것이 있어요? 그것을 이루기 위해 어떤 준비가 필요한지 말해 봅시다.

Is there something you're hoping for these days? Discuss what kind of preparations are needed to realize that hope.

(27) 참새

가을 지난 마당은 하이얀 종이
참새들이 글씨를 공부하지요.

째액째액 입으론 받아 읽으며
두 발로는 글씨를 연습하지요.

하루 종일 글씨를 공부하여도
짹 자 한 자밖에 더 못 쓰는걸.

Background Knowledge   Along with other poems, *Sparrows* takes place in the yard of Yoon Dong-ju's birthplace, in Yongjeong, North Gando Province. Yoon Dong-ju grew up in Yongjeong with Song Mong-gyu. Song Mong-gyu was Yoon Dong-ju's paternal cousin, who made his literary debut first, and left to study abroad with him in Japan, where he gathered students who came to study there into the independence movement, and had a large impact on Yoon Dong-ju's life. If you watch the black-and-white movie *Dongju: The Portrait of a Poet* (2016), you can appreciate Song Mong-gyu's fight for independence and Yoon Dong-ju's poetic sensibilities.

MP3 27

Sparrows

The yard after autumn has passed is white paper,
And the sparrows are learning to write their letters.

"Tweet, tweet," they read out with their mouths,
And practice writing their letters with two feet.

Though they spend the whole day learning to write their letters,
They can't write anything but "tweet."

Vocabulary

가을 autumn	받다 to receive
마당 yard	읽다 to read
하얗다 to be white	발 foot
종이 paper	연습하다 to practice
글씨 letters, writing	하루 종일 all day, the whole day
짹짹 tweet tweet	

V는걸

A sentence-final ending that expresses that the present fact is different from already known information or expectations. It expresses a gentle rebuttal, or regret or admiration about something that has passed. When expressing the past tense, -았는걸 is used; with an adjective, DV(으)ㄴ걸 is used; and with a noun, N인걸 is used.

> **Ex** 그것 참 좋은걸. That's really great.
>
> 아기가 춥겠는걸? The baby must be cold.
>
> 짐이 너무 많은걸. I have too much luggage.
>
> 밤새 눈이 많이 왔는걸! It snowed a lot overnight!
>
> 그때는 아직 서로 이름도 모르는 사이였는걸.
> At the time, we didn't even know each other's names yet.

1 시에서 강조된 부분의 문법을 분석해 보세요. 어떤 단어와 문법이 쓰였습니까?

Look at the emphasized part of the poem and analyze its grammar. Which words and grammar were used?

	=		+		+		+	

2 다음 표현을 써서 문장을 완성하세요.

Write out the following expressions and complete the sentences.

V는걸

(가) 윤동주　　형, 영화 보러 갈래?

　　송몽규　　난 너랑 밥 먹고 싶은걸. ___________

(나) 윤동주　　그럼 중국집에 갈까?

　　송몽규　　___________

(다) 윤동주　　삼겹살 2인분 시킬까?

　　송몽규　　___________

(라) 윤동주　　이제 고기는 그만 먹고 냉면을 시킬까?

　　송몽규　　___________

(마) 윤동주   형, 공부하러 고향을 떠난 거 후회는 안 해?

송몽규   ____

(바) 윤동주   우리 고향집 마당에 가을이면 참새들이 날아오던 거 기억나?

송몽규   ____

3 처음 한국어 공부를 하던 때가 생각나요? 한글 자모 24자를 배우는 데 시간이 얼마나 걸렸는지 말해 봅시다.

Do you remember when you first started studying Korean? Discuss how long it took you to learn the 24 Korean letters.

Vocabulary ____

자모 a letter (in an alphabet)   후회 regret

(28) 남쪽 하늘

제비는 두 나래를 가지었다.
스산한 가을날 ——

어머니의 젖가슴이 그리운,
서리 내리는 저녁 ——
어린 영혼은 쪽빛 나래의 향수를 타고
남쪽 하늘에 떠돌 뿐 —

MP3 28

Southern Sky

The swallow had two wings.
A dreary autumn day –

Longing for its mother's breast
On an evening when frost has fallen –
A young soul rides on indigo wings of nostalgia,
Simply hovering in the southern sky –

Vocabulary

남쪽 south, southern
제비 swallow
나래 wing
스산하다 to be dreary
젖가슴 breast, bosom
서리 frost

내리다 to fall
영혼 spirit, soul
쪽빛 indigo
향수 nostalgia, homesickness
떠돌다 to hover

(N1이/가) V1는,

A comma in a sentence indicates a distant (non-adjacent) modification by a relative clause. Typically, adjectives take the endings -은/ㄴ/을 depending on whether the stem ends in a consonant and whether the meaning is speculative, while verbs take -은/는/을 depending on tense (past, present, or future) to modify a following noun directly. However, if the noun being modified does not appear immediately after the relative clause, a comma (,) is used after the clause to show that the noun being described is located elsewhere in the sentence.

> (Ex) 카페 직원이 반쯤 남**은**, 탁자 위의 커피 잔을 치우고 있다.
> The café employee is clearing away the half-emptied cup of coffee on the table.
>
> 날마다 저녁 6시면 울리**는**, 오래된 성당의 종소리가 아름답다.
> The sound of the old cathedral bell that rigs every evening at 6 is beautiful.
>
> 친구 집에서 처음 먹어 **본**, 친구 어머니께서 끓여 주신 떡국 맛을 잊을 수 없다.
> I can't forget the taste of the rice cake soup my friend's mother made for me, which I ate for the first time at his house.

1 시에서 강조된 부분의 문법을 분석해 보세요. 어떤 단어와 문법이 쓰였습니까?

Look at the emphasized part of the poem and analyze its grammar. Which words and grammar were used?

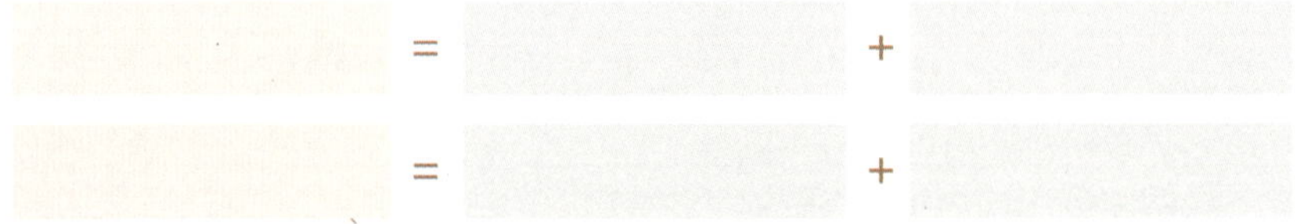

2 쉼표가 필요한 단어에 밑줄을 긋고 쉼표를 찍어 봅시다.

Underline the words that need a comma and then add a comma.

(가) 이번 여름에는 꼭 <u>시원한</u>, 충무로 평양냉면을 먹으러 가자.

(나) 윤동주는 대한민국을 대표하는 한국 사람이 제일 좋아하는 시인 중 한 명이다.

(다) 〈남쪽 하늘〉은 1935년 10월 평양에서 쓰인 서울에 대한 시인의 향수가 잘 드러난 작품이다.

(라) 이 시에서 제비의 두 날개는 가고 싶은 곳에 마음대로 가고 싶어 하는 윤동주의 간절한 바람을 나타낸다.

3 가을이 되면 그리워지는 사람이 있나요? 왜 그 사람이 가을에 특별히 더 그리워지는지 말해 봅시다.

Is there someone you miss in the autumn? Discuss why you miss that person more in the autumn in particular.

Vocabulary

충무로 Chungmuro (a street in Seoul famous for art, culture, and film)
평양 Pyeongyang (the capital of North Korea)
대표하다 to represent
제비 swallow

날개 wing
마음대로 as one pleases
간절하다 to be earnest
바람 hope, wish
나타내다 to appear, to express

(29) 밤

외양간 당나귀
아—ㅇ 앙 외마디 울음 울고,

당나귀 소리에
으— 아 아 애기 소스라쳐 깨고,

등잔에 불을 다오.

아버지는 당나귀에게
짚을 한 키 담아 주고,

어머니는 애기에게
젖을 한 모금 먹이고,

밤은 다시 고요히 잠드오.

MP3 29

Night

The donkey in the barn
Brays out a single "hee haw!"

And at the donkey's sound,
The baby wakes and cries out, "Wa-ah!"

Light the oil lamp.

Father gives the donkey
A bale of hay,

And mother gives the baby
Some milk from her breast,

And the night falls silently to sleep again.

Vocabulary

외양간 barn	달다 to heat, to light
당나귀 donkey	짚 straw, hay
외마디 a single word or sound	키 a tool used for drying grain breast
울다 to cry, to make (a sound)	젖 a drop
애기 baby	모금 a sip
소스라치다 to be startled	고요히 silently
깨다 to wake up	잠들다 to fall asleep
등잔 oil lamp	

1 시에서 강조된 부분의 문법을 분석해 보세요. 어떤 단어와 문법이 쓰였습니까?

Look at the emphasized part of the poem and analyze its grammar. Which words and grammar were used?

2 사동 표현을 사용해서 엄마가 무엇을 하는지 쓰십시오.

Use a causative expression to write what the mother is doing.

(가)

엄마가 아이를 씻겨요.

(나)

(다)

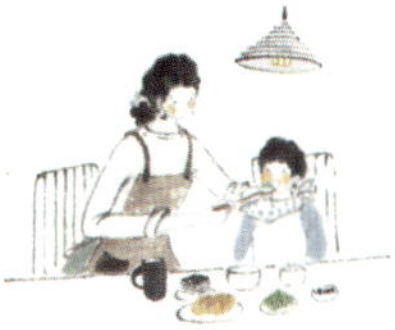

____

(라)

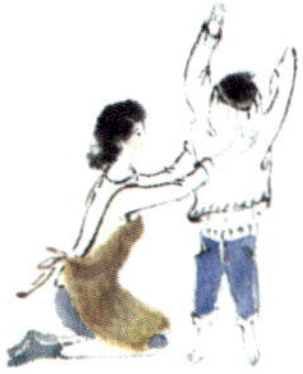

____

(마)

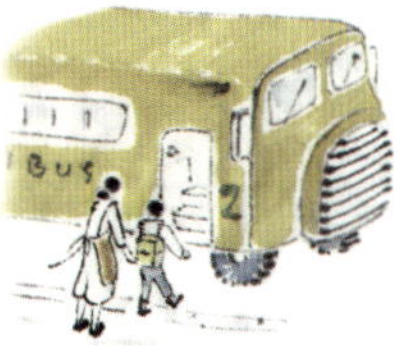

____

(바)

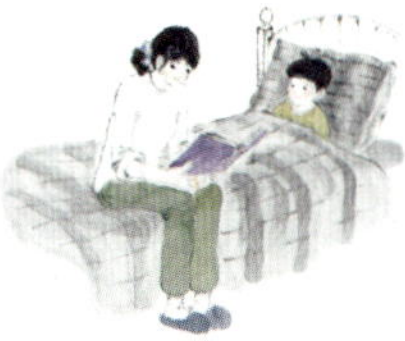

____

3 여러분은 나보다 약한 누군가를 도와준 경험이 있어요? 언제 누구에게 어떤 도움을 주었나요?

Have you ever helped someone who was weaker than you? What kind of help did you give to whom, and when?

⟨30⟩ 눈 감고 간다

태양을 사모하는 아이들아
별을 사랑하는 아이들아

밤이 어두웠는데
눈 감고 가거라.

가진 바 씨앗을
뿌리면서 가거라.

발부리에 돌이 차이거든
감았던 눈을 와짝 떠라.

MP3 30

Go with your eyes closed

Hey, children who adore the sun,
Hey, children who adore the stars,

Night has grown dark,
So close your eyes and go.

The seeds you hold in your hands
Scatter them as you go.

If you are tripped up by a stone,
Open wide your eyes which were closed.

Vocabulary ______________________________

감다 to close
태양 sun
사모하다 to adore
씨앗 seed
뿌리다 to spread, to scatter

발부리 the tips of one's toes
돌이 차이다 to trip over a stone
와짝 wide
뜨다 to open

V거든

A connective ending meaning "if something is true," or "if something turns out to be true."

Ex 선생님을 만나**거든** 내 안부도 전해 줘. If you meet our teacher, greet them for me, too.

할아버지께서 편찮으시**거든** 내게 꼭 알려라. If grandfather is sick, make sure to tell me.

혹시 내일도 시위가 예정되어 있**거든** 지하철을 이용해라.
If there's a protest scheduled for tomorrow, take the subway.

약을 먹어도 감기가 낫지 않**거든** 모레 다시 병원에 가 봐라.
If your cold doesn't get better even after taking medicine, go back to the hospital the day after tomorrow.

1 시에서 강조된 부분의 문법을 분석해 보세요. 어떤 단어와 문법이 쓰였습니까?
Look at the emphasized part of the poem and analyze its grammar. Which words and grammar were used?

  =   +   +

2 관계있는 것을 연결한 뒤 다음 표현을 써서 문장을 완성하세요.
Connect the items that are related, then write out the following expressions and complete the sentences.

V거든

(가) 찌개가 짜다	① 한 그릇 더 먹을래?
(나) 레몬이 시다	② 소금을 좀 넣으세요.
(다) 떡볶이가 맵다	③ 탄산수에 넣어서 마셔 봐.
(라) 약이 많이 쓰다	④ 초콜릿을 한 조각 드세요.
(마) 삼계탕이 싱겁다	⑤ 우유를 한 모금 드셔 보세요.
(바) 국이 그렇게 맛있다	⑥ 물을 한 그릇 더 붓고 끓이자.

(가)

(나)

(다)

(라)

(마)

(바)

3 동요 '태양을 사모하는 아이들아'는 윤동주의 시 두 편을 합쳐 가사로 만들고 거기에 멜로디를 입힌 노래입니다. 여러분도 이 노래를 듣고 따라 불러 보세요.

The children's song "Children Who Adore the Sun" was made by combining two of Yoon Dong-ju's poems to make the lyrics, and then adding a melody. Listen to the song and try singing along.

태양을 사모하는 아이들아

31 새벽이 올 때까지

다들 죽어가는 사람들에게
검은 옷을 입히시오.

다들 살아가는 사람들에게
흰 옷을 입히시오.

그리고 한 침대에
가지런히 잠을 재우시오.

다들 울거들랑
젖을 먹이시오.

이제 새벽이 오면
나팔 소리 들려올 게외다.

Background Knowledge Beginning in May 1941, when this poem was written, Yoon Dong-ju moved out of his school's dormitory and took a room in the house of novelist Kim Song. In this year, Yoon Dong-ju avidly read works of foreign literature by Rilke, Valéry, Gide, and more, and began to study French.

Until the Dawn Arrives

Please dress in black clothing
All those who are dying.

Please dress in white clothing
All those who are living.

And in one bed,
Put them to sleep in a neat row.

When all cry out,
Give a breast to suckle

And now, when the dawn arrives,
The sound of the trumpet will be heard.

Vocabulary ______________________________

새벽 dawn	재우다 to put to bed
검다 to be black	젖 breast
입히다 to dress (someone)	나팔 trumpet
가지런히 in order	들리다 to be heard

A connective ending that expresses the meaning "if something is true," or "if something turns out to be true," mainly used together with a request ending. This is an expression that combines the ending -거든 with the particle 을랑. 을랑 is used between people who are close, with whom casual speech can be used, and has the meaning that something is limited to certain special situations. When -거들랑 is used at the end of a sentence as sentence-closing ending, it has the function of an additional explanation that teaches content that is unknown to the listener.

> (Ex) 사실은 내가 귤을 제일 좋아하**걸랑**. Actually, I like tangerines best.
>
> 그 시간에 우리는 카페에 있었**거들랑**. We were at a café at that time.
>
> 어려운 일이 생기**걸랑** 바로 연락해라. If something difficult happens, contact me right away.
>
> 고향에 가**거들랑** 부모님께 내 안부도 전해라.
> If you go to your hometown, give your parents my best.

1 시에서 강조된 부분의 문법을 분석해 보세요. 어떤 단어와 문법이 쓰였습니까?

Look at the emphasized part of the poem and analyze its grammar. Which words and grammar were used?

	=	+	+

2 다음 표현을 써서 문장을 완성하세요.

Write out the following expressions and complete the sentences.

V거들랑

(가) 고궁에 가게 되다 / 꼭 한복을 입고 가 봐라.

(나) 관광지에서 길을 잘 모르겠다 / 길 찾기 앱을 이용해 봐.

(다) 밤에 잠 잘 숙소가 없다 / 주변 찜질방을 검색해 보지 그래.

(라) 여행을 재미있게 하고 싶다 / 미리 한국말을 좀 배워 가지고 가.

(마) 서울에서 대중교통으로 이동할 계획이다 / 교통 카드를 사서 쓰는 게 좋아.

(바) 한국 사람과 함께 식사할 기회가 생기다 / 윗사람이 수저를 들 때까지 기다리도록 해.

(가) 고궁에 가게 되거들랑 꼭 한복을 입고 가 봐라.

(나)

(다)

(라)

(마)

(바)

3 아래 편지를 읽고, 여러분도 부탁할 말이 있는 사람에게 편지를 써 봅시다.
Read the letter below, and then write a letter to someone you're asking a favor of.

아이가 태어나거들랑 예쁜 이름을 지어 주시오.
한 살이 되거들랑 돌잔치를 크게 해 주시오.
초등학교에 들어가거들랑 처음 한 달은 날마다 교문까지
데려다주시오. 엄마보다 더 좋아하는 친구가 생기거들랑
항상 이해해 주시오. 우리 아이가 결혼을 하거들랑
그래도 항상 그들도 우리처럼 서로 사랑하며 살도록 도와주시오.

32 비행기

머리의 프로펠러가
방앗간 풍차보다
더 ─ 빨리 돈다.

땅에서 오를 때보다
하늘에 높이 떠서는
빠르지 못하다.
숨결이 찬 모양이야.*

비행기는 ──
새처럼 나래를
펄럭거리지 못한다.
그리고, 늘 ──
소리를 지른다
숨이 찬가 봐.**

Airplane

The propeller at its head
Turns faster, faster
Than the blades of the windmill.

As when it climbs up from the ground,
Once it flies high in the sky,
It is no longer as fast.
Perhaps it is short of breath.

The airplane –
Like a bird, its wings
Cannot flap.
And it always –
Shrieks out loud.
It must be short of breath.

Vocabulary

비행기 airplane	숨결 breath, breathing
방앗간 mill	모양 shape, appearance
풍차 windmill	나래(날개) wing
돌다 to turn	펄럭거리다 to flap
오르다 to climb	늘 always
뜨다 to fly, to float	숨이 차다 to be short of breath

AV는 모양이다

A sentence-closing ending that indicates a guess. When combined with the past form of a verb or with an adjective, AV은/ㄴ 모양이다 is used. AV나/DV은가/N인가 보다/싶다 also indicates a guess, but AV는 모양이다 is used when making slightly more specific guesses based on things you can see or hear.

(Ex) 친구 얼굴이 어두운 걸 보니 무슨 일이 **생긴 모양이다.**
Seeing how my friend's face looks dark, something must have happened.

저 혼자 그 정도면 충분하지 않**은가 싶어서** 그 방을 계약했습니다.
I thought it would be enough for me, living alone, so I rented that room.

맨날 놀면서도 시험 성적이 좋은 걸 보면 그 친구는 머리가 **좋은가 보다.**
Seeing as how they play every day and still get good grades on their test, that friend must be smart.

1 시에서 강조된 부분의 문법을 분석해 보세요. 어떤 단어와 문법이 쓰였습니까?
Look at the emphasized part of the poem and analyze its grammar. Which words and grammar were used?

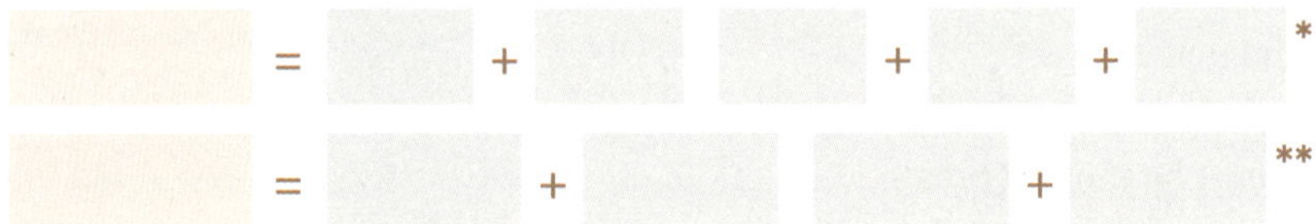

2 다음 표현을 써서 문장을 완성하세요.
Write out the following expressions and complete the sentences.

AV는 모양이야.　　**AV나/DV은가/N인가 봐.**

(가)

아기가 아픈 모양이야. / 아기가 아픈가 봐.

(나)

(다)

(라)

(마)

---

3 주변을 둘러보세요. 누가 있어요? 그들이 지금 어떤 기분인 것 같은지 추측해 봅시다.

Look around you. Who do you see? Take a guess as to what you think they might be feeling right now.

Grammar Tip

***-야:** (Written after the stem 이다 or 아니다) A sentence-closing ending used when describing or asking about a fact.

Ex 이게 뭐야? What's this?　　　　　　　　그는 참 좋은 사람이야. He's a very good person.
　　그건 사실이 아니야. That isn't true.

****-어/아/여:** A sentence-closing ending that indicates a description of a fact or a question, order, or suggestion.

Ex 나는 지금 밥 먹어. I'm eating right now.　　　아이, 예뻐. How pretty.
　　뭐가 그리 우스워? What's so funny?

（33） 창구멍

바람 부는 새벽에 장터 가시는
우리 아빠 뒷자취 보고 싶어서
침을 발라 뚫어 논 작은 창구멍
아롱아롱 아침 해 비치웁니다.

눈 내리는 저녁에 나무 팔러 간
우리 아빠 오시나 기다리다가
혀끝으로 뚫어 논 작은 창구멍
살랑살랑 찬바람 날아듭니다.

Background Knowledge This poem, "The Window's Opening," was adapted in 1938 from "Sunlight·Wind." Let's compare the two poems and see what similarities and differences in feeling we find.

MP3 33

The Window's Opening

Because I want to see my father's silhouette from behind
As he goes to market in the blustery dawn –
Through the small window's opening that I pierced with spit,
The morning sun shines, glittering, glittering.

Because I want to wait for my father coming home
Once he's gone to sell wood in the snowy evening –
Through the small window's opening I pierced with the tip of my tongue,
The cold air blows, gently, gently.

Vocabulary

구멍 hole, opening
새벽 dawn
장터 market
뒷자취 rear silhouette
침 spit
바르다 to apply
뚫다 to pierce

아롱아롱 glittering
해 sun
비치다 to shine
혀끝 the tip of a tongue
살랑살랑 gently
차다 to be cold
날아들다 to come in, to fly in

AV어/아 놓다

An auxiliary verb that indicates that after the action of the verb has completed, the result of that action is maintained.

> **Ex** 더우니 문을 **열어 놓아라**. It's hot, so open the door [and leave it open].
>
> 보고서는 어제 벌써 다 **써 놓았다.**
> I already wrote the whole report yesterday [and it is finished and remains written].
>
> 꽃병에 꽂**아 논** 꽃이 일주일 만에 다 시들었다.
> The flowers I put [and left] in the vase all withered in just a week.
>
> 탁자 위에 벗**어 놓았던** 모자를 들어서 머리에 썼다.
> I took the hat that had been taken off and left on the table, and put it on my head.

1 시에서 강조된 부분의 문법을 분석해 보세요. 어떤 단어와 문법이 쓰였습니까?

Look at the emphasized part of the poem and analyze its grammar. Which words and grammar were used?

2 내일 생일을 맞는 가족을 위해서 어떤 준비를 했어요? 다음 표현을 써서 문장을 완성하세요.

What preparations were made for the family member celebrating a birthday tomorrow? Write out the following expressions and complete the sentences.

AV어/아 놓았어요

(가) 카드를 쓰다   ➡ ________________________________

(나) 잡채를 하다   ➡ ________________________________

(다) 과일을 깎다   ➡ ________________________________

(라) 케이크를 사다   ➡ ________________________________

(마) 미역국을 끓이다   ➡ ________________________________

(바) 창문에 풍선을 달다   ➡ ________________________________

3 집에서 어느 공간을 제일 좋아해요? 마음에 드는 그 공간에 자신이 특별히 무엇을 해 놓았는지,
왜 그렇게 해 놓았는지 말해 봅시다.

What is your favorite space in your house? Discuss what in particular you've put in that
space and why you've put it there.

풍선을 달다 to put up a balloon

(34) 유언

훠 — ㄴ한 방에
유언은 소리 없는 입놀림.

—— 바다에 진주 캐러 **갔다는** 아들
　　해녀와 사랑을 **속삭인다는** 맏아들
　　이 밤에사 돌아오나 내다봐라 ——

평생 외롭던 아버지의 운명(殞命)
감기우는 눈에 슬픔이 어린다.

외딴집에 개가 짖고
휘영청 달이 문살에 흐르는 밤.

MP3 34

Last Testament

In the bright, bright room,
His last testament is a soundless moving of lips.

— My son, who they say went searching for pearls in the ocean,
My first son, who speaks whispers or love with a diver woman,
Look out into the night to see if he is coming. —

The final fate of a father who spent his whole life lonely,
In eyes slowly closing, sorrow lingers.

A dog barks in a far-off house,
And bright moonlight flows over the panes of the door this evening.

Vocabulary

유언 will, last testament	내다보다 to look out, to look ahead
훤하다 to be bright	평생 one's whole life
입놀림 movement of one's lips	운명 destiny, fate
진주 pearl	외딴집 an isolated house
캐다 to mine, to dig for	짖다 to bark, to cry
해녀 diver woman	휘영청 bright
속삭이다 to whisper	문살 strip separating panes of a door or window
맏아들 oldest son	

V다는 N

-다는, which modifies a noun, is a shortened version of -다고 하는, and is an expression of indirect quotation used when conveying information that you heard from someone else. If the thing you heard is a question, -냐는 is used; if it's a request, -으라는 is used; and if it's a suggestion, -자는 is used. For the sake of the person who made the request, it's good to omit adverbs like 좀 (a bit, just) and summarize the information that you are conveying.

Ex 동호회를 만들**자는** 얘기 들었어? Did you hear about starting a club?

사장님이 직접 서빙을 하겠**다는** 말을 듣고 모두 놀랐다.
Everyone was surprised to hear the boss say that he'd do the serving himself.

이번 주말에 중부 지방에 태풍이 지나갈 거**라는** 뉴스를 들었다.
I heard the news that a typhoon will pass through the central part of the country this weekend.

1 시에서 강조된 부분의 문법을 분석해 보세요. 어떤 단어와 문법이 쓰였습니까?

Look at the emphasized part of the poem and analyze its grammar. Which words and grammar were used?

	=		+		+		+	
	=		+		+		+	

2 다음 표현을 써서 문장을 완성하세요.

Write out the following expressions and complete the sentences.

V다는 N을/를 들었다.

(가) 돈을 좀 빌려주세요.　　　　　　　　　　① 질문

(나) 내일은 비가 올 겁니다.　　　　　　　　　② 조언

(다) 한국 시를 읽어 봤어요?　　　　　　　　　③ 약속

(라) 다시는 거짓말을 하지 않겠습니다.　　　　④ 부탁

(마) 영화를 보면서 한국어 공부를 해 보세요.　⑤ 일기예보

(가) 돈을 빌려 달라는 부탁을 들었다.

(나)

(다)

(라)

(마)

3 여러분은 조언을 들어 본 적이 있나요? 그 중에서 어떤 조언이 가장 도움이 되었는지 말해
봅시다.

Have you ever taken someone's advice? Discuss the advice you've taken that has helped
you the most.

Vocabulary

조언 advice

35 아우의 인상화

붉은 이마에 싸늘한 달이 서리어
아우의 얼굴은 슬픈 그림이다.

발걸음을 멈추어
살그머니 앳된 손을 잡으며
"너는 자라 무엇이 되려니"

"사람이 되지"
아우의 서러운 진정코 서러운 대답이다.

슬며 ― 시 잡았던 손을 놓고
아우의 얼굴을 다시 들여다본다.

싸늘한 달이 붉은 이마에 젖어
아우의 얼굴은 슬픈 그림이다.

Background Knowledge   An impression (portrait) refers to a picture painted in the impressionist style. Impressionism was a trend in modern art that arose in the latter half of the 19th century in France, with the goal of boldly and subjectively expressing the artist's momentary impression rather than reproducing an object accurately as it is. The result was a rejection of the true color of an item, and the popularization of a style that captured the momentary colors of an object that, in the sunlight, appears different from moment to moment. Representative artists include Degas, Renoir, Manet, Monet, etc.

MP3 35

Portrait of a Younger Brother

Moonlight frosted icily on his ruddy forehead,
My younger brother's face is a sad picture.

I stopped walking
And gently took hold of his childish hand,
"What do you want to be when you grow up?"

"A person, of course."
My younger brother's sad, oh so sad reply.

Gently, gently, I released the hand I had held
And looked into his face again.

His ruddy forehead soaked in cold moonlight,
My younger brother's face is a sad picture.

Vocabulary ____

아우 younger brother	살그머니 gently, furtively
인상화 impression	앳되다 to be young, to be child-like
이마 forehead	서럽다 to be sad
싸늘하다 to be icy, to be cold	진정코 very, truly
서리다 to fog up, to frost, to mist	슬며시 gently, secretly
발걸음 step	들여다보다 to look into
멈추다 to stop	

1 시에서 강조된 부분의 문법을 분석해 보세요. 어떤 단어와 문법이 쓰였습니까?

Look at the emphasized part of the poem and analyze its grammar. Which words and grammar were used?

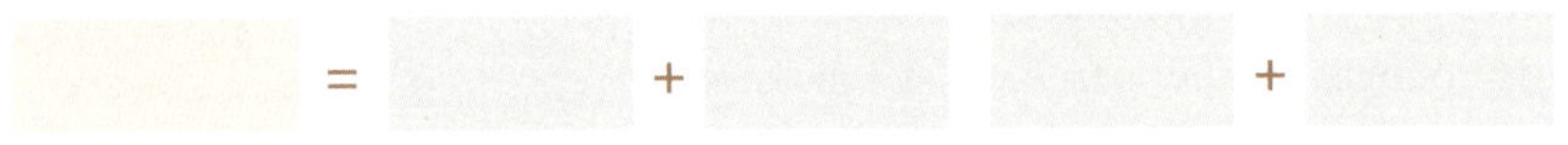

2 친구의 질문에 대한 대답으로 알맞은 말을 고르십시오.

Choose the correct answer to your friend's question.

V지.

(가) 동아리 신입생 환영회가 언제지? ·

· ① 저녁 7시잖아.

(나) 몇 시지? ·

· ② 다음 주 금요일.

(다) 어디지? ·

· ③ 졸리와 산디가 선약이 있다고 했어.

(라) 못 온다고 한 사람이 누구누구지? ·

· ④ 너 지난번 준비 회의 내내 딴짓 했지?

(마) 나는 왜 하나도 생각이 안 나지? ·

· ⑤ 1차 모임은 동아리 방에서 하고 2차로 학교 앞 한식집에 가기로 했어.

3 여러분은 '인상화'에 대해 알고 있나요? 만약 자신의 얼굴을 '인상화'로 그린다면 어느 부분을 강조해서 어떤 색으로 그릴 것 같아요? 직접 그림을 그려 봅시다.

Do you know about portraits? If you were to draw a portrait of your face, which colors would you use to emphasize which parts? Try drawing it for yourself.

(36) 사랑스런 추억

봄이 오던 아침, 서울 어느 쪼그만 정거장에서
희망과 사랑처럼 기차를 기다려

나는 플랫폼에 간신한 그림자를 떨어트리고
담배를 피웠다.

내 그림자는 담배 연기 그림자를 날리고
비둘기 한 떼가 부끄러울 것도 없이
나래 속을 속, 속, 햇빛에 비춰, 날았다.

기차는 아무 새로운 소식도 없이
나를 멀리 실어다 주어

봄은 다 가고 —— 동경 교외 어느 조용한 하숙방에서, 옛 거리에 남은 나를
희망과 사랑처럼 그리워한다.

오늘도 기차는 몇 번이나 무의미하게 지나가고

오늘도 나는 누구를 기다려 정거장 가까운
언덕에서 서성거릴 게다.

—— 아아 젊음은 오래 거기 남아 있거라.

Background Knowledge

This poem was written on paper from Rikkyo University. In April 1942, Yoon Dong-ju entered literature department of Tokyo's Rikkyo University as an English literature major; he wrote the 5 poems *White Shadow, Flowing Street, Beloved Memory, A Poem Easily Written*, and *Spring* on paper from Rikkyo University and sent them to his friend Kang Cheo-joong in Seoul. In October 1942, Yoon Dong-ju moved to the English literature department of Doshisha University and continued his studies. On July 14, 1943, before returning home for his summer break, he was arrested and charged by Shimogamo Police Station in Kyoto for violating the law on "preservation of public order," received a sentence of 2 years, and was imprisoned in Fukuoka Prison, but he died on February 16, 1945, at the young age of 27.

MP3 36

Beloved Memory

On a morning when spring approached, at some small little station in Seoul,
Waiting for a train, as if waiting for hope or for love,

I cast a slender shadow on the platform
And smoked a cigarette.

My shadow blew out a shadow of cigarette smoke,
And a flock of pigeons unabashedly
Flew off, the sunlight shining on the inside, inside, inside of their wings.

The train, bringing no new news,
Takes me far.

Spring has passed – In some quiet boarding house room in a Tokyo suburb, I long,
like for hope or for love, for what's left of me on those streets from my past.

Today, again, the trains pass by several times without meaning,

And today, again, I'll pace the hill nearby the station, waiting for someone.

— Oh, youth, linger on there long.

Vocabulary

추억 memory	떼 flock, pack
쪼그맣다 to be small, to be little	부끄럽다 to be shy, to be ashamed
정거장 station, stop	햇빛 sunlight
희망 hope	비추다 to shine
사랑 love	새롭다 to be new
간신하다 to be slender	소식 news
담배를 피우다 to smoke a cigarette	멀리 far
연기 smoke	싣다 to take aboard, to load
날리다 to fly off	교외 suburb

N처럼

A case-marking particle that indicates that something is similar or identical in shape. Used when emphasizing the similar properties of N1 and N2.

Ex 누나는 천사**처럼** 착하다. My older sister is as kind as an angel.

햇빛이 폭포**처럼** 쏟아졌다. The sunlight streamed down like a waterfall.

네 눈동자가 별**처럼** 반짝인다. Your eyes sparkle like stars.

1 시에서 강조된 부분의 문법을 분석해 보세요. 어떤 단어와 문법이 쓰였습니까?

Look at the emphasized part of the poem and analyze its grammar. Which words and grammar were used?

[   ] = [   ] + [   ]

2 다음 표현을 써서 문장을 완성하세요.

Write out the following expressions and complete the sentences.

N처럼

(가) 눈　　　　　　　　　　　　　① 빨간색 립스틱을 발랐다.

(나) 체리　　　　　　　　　　　　② 파란 가을 하늘이 참 높기도 하다.

(다) 칠흑　　　　　　　　　　　　③ 하얀 강아지가 눈 위에서 뛰놀고 있다.

(라) 금덩어리　　　　　　　　　　④ 노란 해가 석양빛 바다 위로 떨어진다.

(마) 에메랄드　　　　　　　　　　⑤ 까만 밤하늘에 별 하나가 유난히 반짝거린다.

(가) 눈처럼 하얀 강아지가 눈 위에서 뛰놀고 있다.

(나)

(다)

(라)

(마)

3 여러분은 기차를 타고 어디에 가 봤나요? 거기에서 무엇을 했나요? 그날의 느낌이 어땠는지 말해 봅시다.

Where have you taken a train to? What did you do there? Discuss how you felt that day.

Vocabulary

칠흑 pitch dark, pitch black

금덩어리 a nugget of gold

입술 lips

바르다 to apply, to spread

새해 new year

석양빛 evening sunlight

까맣다 to be black, to be dark

유난히 especially

반짝거리다 to twinkle, to sparkle

⟨37⟩ 코스모스

청초한 코스모스는
오직 하나인 나의 아가씨

달빛이 싸늘히 추운 밤이면
옛 소녀가 못 견디게 그리워
코스모스 핀 정원으로 찾아간다.

코스모스는
귀또리 울음에도 수줍어지고

코스모스 앞에 선 나는
어렸을 적처럼 부끄러워지나니

내 마음은 코스모스의 마음이요
코스모스의 마음은 내 마음이다.

Cosmos

The elegant cosmos
Is my one and only young lady.

On a cold night of icy moonlight,
When I cannot bear my longing for my girl of old,
I go to the garden where the cosmos have bloomed.

The cosmos,
At the chirp of the crickets, grow shy,

And I, stood before the cosmos,
Grow bashful as when I was young.

My heart is the heart of the cosmos.
The heart of the cosmos is my heart.

Vocabulary

청초하다 to be elegant
견디다 to withstand, to bear

그립다 to miss, to long for
수줍다 to be shy

V1었을 적처럼 V2나니

적 is a dependent noun used after a noun or the endings (으)ㄴ or (으)ㄹ, with the meaning of a time in which an action continues or a state occurs, or a time that has passed. -나니, is an old expression that, like -기 때문에, explains that the proceeding phrase is the cause, basis, or prerequisite of the phrase that follows.

> (Ex) 아이 **적**에 있었던 일이다. It's something that happened when I was a child.
>
> 나는 고향을 떠난 뒤에 편히 잠을 자 본 **적**이 없다.
> I haven't slept comfortably once since leaving my hometown.
>
> 이 옷은 우리 어머니가 처녀 **적**에 입으셨던 옷이다.
> These clothes are the clothes my mother wore when she was a young woman.
>
> 금방 잠이 **들 적**도 있고 잠이 안 와서 밤새 누워만 **있을 적**도 있다.
> There are times when I fall asleep right away, and times when I can't sleep and just lie awake all night.

1 시에서 강조된 부분의 문법을 분석해 보세요. 어떤 단어와 문법이 쓰였습니까?

Look at the emphasized part of the poem and analyze its grammar. Which words and grammar were used?

2 다음 표현을 써서 문장을 완성하세요.

Write out the following expressions and complete the sentences.

V었을/았을 적처럼 VL나니.

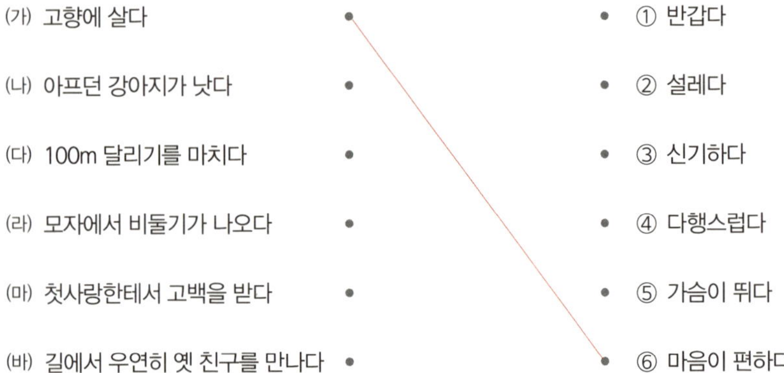

(가) 고향에 살았을 적처럼 마음이 편하나니.

(나)

(다)

(라)

(마)

(바)

3 여러분은 코스모스 꽃을 본 적이 있나요? 그때 누구와 있었고 어떤 기분이었는지 말해 봅시다.
Have you seen cosmos flowers before? Discuss who you were with and how you felt at that time.

(Ex) 코스모스 밭에 들어섰을 때 어릴 때 처음 놀이공원에 갔을 적처럼 설레었나니.

(38) 자화상

산모퉁이를 돌아 논가 외딴 우물을 홀로 찾아가선
가만히 들여다봅니다.

우물 속에는 달이 밝고 구름이 흐르고
하늘이 펼치고 파아란 바람이 불고 가을이 있습니다.

그리고 한 사나이가 있습니다.
어쩐지 그 사나이가 미워져 돌아갑니다.

돌아가다 생각하니 그 사나이가 가엾어집니다.
도로 가 들여다보니 사나이는 그대로 있습니다.

다시 그 사나이가 미워져 돌아갑니다.
돌아가다 생각하니 그 사나이가 그리워집니다.

우물 속에는 달이 밝고 구름이 흐르고
하늘이 펼치고 파아란 바람이 불고
가을이 있고 추억처럼 사나이가
있습니다.

MP3 38

Self-Portrait

Turning the foot of the hill, I go alone to the secluded well by the field,
and quietly look inside it.

Within the well, the moon is bright, the clouds drift by, the sky spreads wide,
a blue, blue wind blows, and autumn is there.

And there is a man.
For some reason, I hate the man, and I turn to leave.

I turn to leave, and as I think, I begin to feel sorry for him. When I go back
and look in again, he is still there.

I hate him again, and I turn to leave.
I turn to leave, and as I think, I begin to miss him.

Within the well, the moon is bright, the clouds drift by, the sky spreads wide,
a blue, blue wind blows, autumn is there, and a man, like a reminiscence,
is there as well.

Vocabulary

자화상 self-portrait
산모퉁이 the foot of a hill, the bend in a
　　　mountain
논가 field
외딴 isolated, secluded
우물 well
홀로 alone
가만히 quietly, still

사나이 man
어쩐지 somehow, for some reason
밉다 to hate
돌아가다 to go back, to return
가엽다 to feel sorry for
도로 road
그대로 like that, as is
추억 memory, reminiscence

DV어/아지다

An auxiliary verb that indicates that something takes on the state meant by the adjective stem.

Ex 오랜만에 방이 깨끗**해졌다**. The room has gotten cleaner for the first time in a long time.

생각을 바꾸니 마음이 편**해졌다**. Changing my mind made my heart feel more at ease.

에어컨을 켜니까 방이 금방 시원**해졌다**.
I turned on the air conditioner, so the room quickly got cooler.

얼굴에 팩을 붙였다가 떼니까 피부가 부드러**워졌다**.
When I put a mask pack on my face and took it off, my skin got softer.

1 시에서 강조된 부분의 문법을 분석해 보세요. 어떤 단어와 문법이 쓰였습니까?

Look at the emphasized part of the poem and analyze its grammar. Which words and grammar were used?

	=		+		+	
	=		+		+	
	=		+		+	

2 다음 표현을 써서 문장을 완성하세요.

Write out the following expressions and complete the sentences.

DV어/아졌다.

(가) 졸업을 앞두고	•	•	① 속도가 빠르다
(나) 한국어를 배우고 나서	•	•	② 진로 고민이 깊다
(다) 밤을 새워 게임을 하고서	•	•	③ 한국 친구가 많다
(라) 한국어로 소설책을 읽는	•	•	④ 갑자기 내가 한심하다
(마) 한국어로 시를 읽다니	•	•	⑤ 내 자신이 자랑스럽다

(가) **졸업을 앞두고 진로 고민이 깊어졌다.**

(나) ____

(다) ____

(라) ____

(마) ____

3 자신의 10년 전 사진을 찾아서 지금 모습과 비교해 보세요. 무엇이 달라졌나요?
Find a picture of yourself 10 years ago and compare it to the way you look now. What has changed?

(39) 간판 없는 거리

정거장 플랫폼에
내렸을 때 아무도 없어

다들 손님들뿐
손님 같은 사람들뿐

집집마다 간판이 없어
집 찾을 근심이 없어

빨갛게
파랗게
불붙는 문자도 없어

모퉁이마다
자애로운 헌 와사등에
불을 켜 놓고

손목을 잡으면
다들, 어진 사람들
다들, 어진 사람들

봄, 여름, 가을, 겨울,
순서로 돌아들고

Background Knowledge   On December 27, 1941, Yoon Dong-ju graduated from Yonhi College (Chosen Christian College). At the time, the economic conditions of passengers who traveled by train and people who lit old gas lamps and waited at the store for guests were very different. In the hometown of Yoon Dong-ju, who had studied abroad, there were none of the "lighted letters in red, in blue" (neon signs) that were found everywhere in the city. But even without those signs, there were no worries about being unable to find a house in the familiar streets of his hometown. This poem clearly shows Yoon Dong-ju's affection for the people of his kindly hometown. The uncompleted sentences in the last stanza indicate the endlessly repeating structure of the trains that come into the platform and the passengers that alight from the train throughout the four seasons of spring, summer, autumn, and winter.

A Road Without Signs

Onto the station platform,
I stepped down, but nobody was there.

All only visitors
And people who seem like visitors.

No signs on any of the houses,
No worry about finding any house.

In red,
In blue,
No lighted letters, either.

At each corner,
A kindly old gas lamp
Is left lit.

And if you take them by the wrist,
All of them, kind people,
All of them, kind people.

Spring, summer, autumn, winter,
All come in in their turn.

Vocabulary

간판 sign	자애롭다 to be kindly, to be benevolent
거리 road	헌 old, worn, shabby
근심 worry	와사등 gas lamp
불붙다 to catch alight	손목 wrist
문자 letters	어질다 to be kind, to be virtuous
모퉁이 corner	순서 order, turn

때 is a noun that indicates the time at which a thing or event occurs.
It is used in the form of N 때, like in time nouns such as 방학 때(during vacation), and -을 때 is used when you want to express a state or action that is occurring, while -었을 때 is used to express a state or action that has already completed.

Ex 체했을 **때**는 따뜻한 물을 마시면 좋다.
When your stomach is upset, it's good to drink warm water.

가끔 이유 없이 머리가 아플 **때**가 있다. There are times when my head hurts for no reason.

단어의 뜻을 모를 **때**는 사전을 찾아봐라.
When you don't know the meaning of a word, look it up in the dictionary.

처음 한국에 왔을 **때**는 한국 친구가 한 명도 없었다.
When I first came to Korea, I didn't even have **a single** Korean friend.

1 시에서 강조된 부분의 문법을 분석해 보세요. 어떤 단어와 문법이 쓰였습니까?
Look at the emphasized part of the poem and analyze its grammar. Which words and grammar were used?

	=		+		+	

2 다음 표현을 써서 문장을 완성하세요.
Write out the following expressions and complete the sentences.

V(었/았)을 때

(가) 몇 살 때부터 혼자 기차를 탔어요?

➡ 대학교에 다닐 때부터 혼자 기차를 탔어요.
____

(나) 어느 계절에 거리의 풍경이 제일 예뻐 보이나요?

➡ ____

(다) 역 근처 가게들은 언제 간판에 불을 켜 두나요?

➡ ____

(라) 한글 간판을 본 적이 있어요? 어디에서 봤어요?

➡ ____

(마) 어느 나라에서 본 정거장 플랫폼이 제일 기억에 남아요?

➡ ____

3 여러분 고향에서 제일 유명한 거리는 어디예요? 그 거리에 갔을 때 무엇을 하면 좋은지 추천해 주세요.

Where is the most famous street in your hometown? Recommend something good to do there.

40 십자가

쫓아오던 햇빛인데
지금 교회당 꼭대기
십자가에 걸리었습니다.

첨탑이 저렇게도 높은데
어떻게 올라갈 수 있을까요.

종소리도 들려오지 않는데
휘파람이나 불며 서성거리다가

괴로웠던 사나이
행복한 예수 그리스도에게처럼
십자가가 허락된다면

모가지를 드리우고
꽃처럼 피어나는 피를
어두워 가는 하늘 밑에
조용히 흘리겠습니다.

Background Knowledge   In 1886, Yoon Dong-ju's family moved from North Hamgyeongdo Province to Gando, and in 1900, they settled in the village of Myeongdong. In 1910, the whole family joined the Christian church, and this poem strongly shows that religious influence. Yoon Dong-ju tried to live a life just like the Jesus that he believed in, and showed constant reflection on his hesitation in the face of moral decisions. Just as Jesus revealed the truth that "we must love one another" through his death, Yoon Dong-ju joined the independence movement readily carrying on his shoulder the cross of his poetry written in Hangeul.

MP3 40

Cross

The sunlight that followed me
Now, at the top of the church,
It is hung upon the cross.

The steeple is so high,
How can the sunlight climb up there?

The sound of the bell does not ring out,
And I hover here, whistling,

The man who suffered,
As to the joyful Jesus Christ,
If the cross were granted to me
As it was to him,

I shall bend my neck, and
Blood blossoming like flowers
Under the darkening sky
Shall spill quietly.

Vocabulary

십자가 cross
쫓아오다 to follow, to chase
교회당 church
걸리다 to hang, to be hung
첨탑 steeple
종소리 sound of a bell
휘파람 whistle

불다 to blow, to whistle
서성거리다 to hang around, to hover
괴롭다 to suffer
허락되다 to be permitted
모가지 neck, head
어둡다 to be dark

V다면

A connective ending used when indicating the meaning of being conditional upon an assumed fact. It is also used as a contraction of the indirect speech form -다고 하면, which is used to convey something someone else said. Depending on whether the verb stem has a final consonant, or whether making a request or suggestion, it can be used as -는다면/-ㄴ다면, -(으)라면, or -자면.

> (Ex) 굳이 그렇게 하겠**다면** 말리지 않겠다. If you say you have to do it like that, I won't stop you.
>
> 약을 먹어도 열이 안 떨어진**다면** 큰일이다.
> If your fever isn't going down even though you took medicine, that's a problem.
>
> 나도 너처럼 건강하**다면** 그 여행을 따라갔을 거다.
> If I were as healthy as you, I would've followed along on that trip.
>
> 아침까지 눈이 왔**다면** 출근길이 더 어려웠을 거다.
> If it had snowed until morning, the commute to work would have been more difficult.

1 시에서 강조된 부분의 문법을 분석해 보세요. 어떤 단어와 문법이 쓰였습니까?
Look at the emphasized part of the poem and analyze its grammar. Which words and grammar were used?

2 다음 표현을 써서 문장을 완성하세요.
Write out the following expressions and complete the sentences.

V다면

(가) 로또에 당첨되다   ① 악기 하나를 시작하고 싶다.

(나) 램프의 요정을 만나다   ② 제주도 올레길을 돌아 보자.

(다) 한국어를 잘하게 되다   ③ 고향에 한글 학교를 하나 세우고 싶다.

(라) 남한과 북한이 통일되다   ④ 첫 번째 소원으로 세계 평화를 빌 거야.

(마) 나이가 열 살쯤 어려지다   ⑤ 제일 먼저 아이돌에게 팬레터를 쓸 거다.

(바) 휴가를 열흘쯤 낼 수 있다   ⑥ DMZ를 지나서 평양냉면을 먹으러 갈 거다.

(가) 로또에 당첨된다면 고향에 한글 학교를 하나 세우고 싶다.

(나) ____

(다) ____

(라) ____

(마) ____

(바) ____

3 부러운 사람이 있어요? 그 사람처럼 될 수 있다면 무엇을 하고 싶은지 말해 봅시다.
Is there someone you envy? Discuss what you would want to do if you could become like them.

Vocabulary

로또 lotto	악기 instrument
당첨되다 to win, to be picked	소원 wish
요정 fairy, genie	세계 world
통일 unification	평화 peace
올레길 olle trail (Jeju Island walking trail)	

41 간

바닷가 햇빛 바른 바위 위에
습한 간을 펴서 말리우자.

코카사쓰 산중에서 도망해 온 토끼처럼
둘러리를 빙빙 돌며 간을 지키자.

내가 오래 기르던 여윈 독수리야!
와서 뜯어먹어라, 시름없이
너는 살찌고
나는 여위어야지, 그러나,

거북이야!
다시는 용궁의 유혹에 안 떨어진다.

프로메테우스 불쌍한 프로메테우스
불을 훔친 죄로 목에 맷돌을 달고
끝없이 침전하는 프로메테우스.

Background Knowledge   A commonality between the story *The Rabbit's Liver* and the myth of Prometheus is that both feature a liver. In *The Rabbit's Liver*, the rabbit is tricked by the turtle (or terrapin), has his liver stolen by the Dragon King, and almost dies, but uses lies to escape from this crisis. The Caucasus Mountains are where Prometheus, who appears in Greek and Roman mythology, is chained for the crime of tricking Zeus, stealing fire, and giving it to mankind. The poet included the Caucasus Mountains in the background of the poem and had the rabbit appear, by which he connected the two stories.

MP3 41

Liver

Upon a rock painted with sunlight by the seaside,
Let me spread out my damp liver to dry.

Like a rabbit that fled from the Caucasus Mountains,
Let me circle round and round, protecting my liver.

Gaunt eagle that I've raised for so long!
Come tear at it and eat it up, without a worry.
You must grow fat
And I must grow gaunt. However,

Turtle!
I will not fall to the temptations of the Dragon Palace again.

Prometheus, poor Prometheus.
With a millstone hung from his neck, for the crime of stealing fire,
Prometheus is dragged down ceaselessly.

Vocabulary

간 liver	뜯어먹다 to tear and eat, to gnaw
바르다 to apply, to paint	시름 anxiety, worry
바위 rock	살찌다 to grow fat
습하다 to be damp, to be moist	거북이 turtle
펴다 to spread out	용궁 Dragon Palace (mythical underwater palace)
말리다 to dry	유혹 temptation
도망 flight, flee	떨어지다 to fall
토끼 rabbit	훔치다 to steal
둘러리(둘레) circle, circumference	죄 sin, crime
빙빙 around, circling	목 neck
지키다 to protect	맷돌 millstone
기르다 to raise	달다 to hang, to wear
여위다 to waste away, to grow gaunt	침전하다 to be dragged down, to fall down

AV어라

A sentence-closing ending that indicates an order. When following a stem that ends in the vowels ㅏ, ㅓ, ㅕ, ㅐ, or ㅔ, it is used as just -라; when the verb stem ends with a final consonant, if the stem contains the vowels ㅜ, ㅓ, ㅠ, or ㅕ, -어라 is used, and if the stem contains the vowels ㅗ, ㅏ, ㅛ, or ㅑ, -아라 is used. With N하다 verbs, N해라 is used. In visual media such as books, the form AV(으)라 is also used to convey the meaning of a strong request to the unspecified listener or reader.

(Ex) 너 자신을 알**라**. Know thyself.

질문에 맞게 답**하라**. Answer the question correctly.

다음 빈칸 안에 알맞은 말을 쓰**라**. Write the correct words in the following blanks.

반찬을 가리지 말고 골고루 먹**어라**. Don't be picky with your side dishes; eat them all evenly.

횡단보도를 건널 때는 항상 손을 들고 건**너라**.
When crossing at a crosswalk, always raise your hand and cross the street.

1 시에서 강조된 부분의 문법을 분석해 보세요. 어떤 단어와 문법이 쓰였습니까?

Look at the emphasized part of the poem and analyze its grammar. Which words and grammar were used?

     =   +   +   +   +

2 다음 표현을 써서 문장을 완성하세요.

Write out the following expressions and complete the sentences.

AV어/아/여라

(가) 해야, <u>솟아라, 고운 해야, 모든 어둠 먹고 앳된 얼굴 솟아라.</u> (박두진, 1946. 〈해〉 일부)

(나) 달아, ______________________________

(다) 비야, ______________________________

(라) 나무야, ______________________________

(마) 나비야, ______________________________

3 이 시 <간>에 섞여 있는 두 개의 이야기가 무엇인지 알고 있나요? 왜 윤동주는 두 개의 이야기를 섞어서 제시하고 있을까요?

Do you know what the two stories mixed together in this poem "Liver" are? Why do you think Yoon Dong-ju mixes them together?

귀뚤귀뚤

B2

42 햇빛·바람

손가락에 침 발라
쏘 — ㄱ, 쏙, 쏙
장에 가는 엄마 내다보려

문풍지를
쏘 — ㄱ, 쏙, 쏙

아침에 햇빛이 반짝,
손가락에 침 발라
쏘 — ㄱ, 쏙, 쏙
장에 가신 엄마 돌아오나
문풍지를
쏘 — ㄱ, 쏙, 쏙

저녁에 바람이 솔솔.

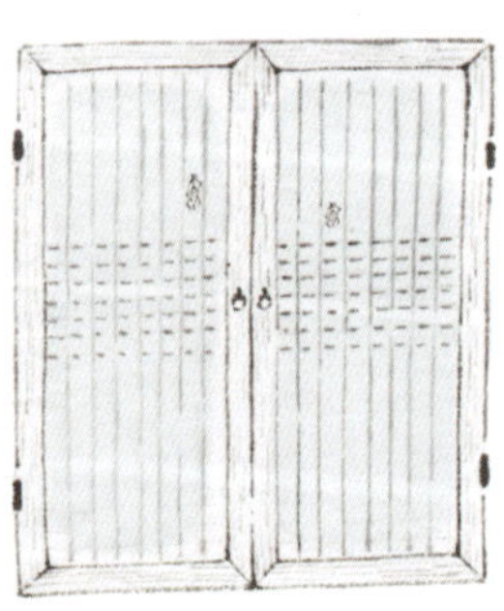

Sunlight · Wind

I wet my finger with spit
And poke it thro — ugh, through, through
To watch Mother going off to market.

The paper of the door
Thro — ugh, through, through.

The sun shining bright in the morning,
I wet my finger with spit
And poke it thro — ugh, through, through
To watch Mother coming back from market.
The paper of the door
Thro — ugh, through, through.

The breeze blowing soft in the evening.

Vocabulary ______________________________________

손가락 finger
침 spit
쏙쏙 through

장 market
솔솔 gently, softly

AV(으)려고

A connective ending that indicates that the speaker has the intention of doing a certain action. Any verb can appear following this ending, so long as it is an action required to achieve that objective. However, the ending AV(으)러, which similarly expresses intent, can only be used when followed by verbs like 가다 and 오다, which indicate movement toward or from a place.

> (Ex) 새 집을 사**려고** 저축을 하고 있다. I'm saving up in order to buy a new house.
>
> 너는 여기서 언제까지 살**려고** 하니? How long do you intend to live here?
>
> 장학금을 타**려고** 두 배로 열심히 공부하는 중이다.
> I'm studying twice as hard in order to win a scholarship.
>
> 내일 아침에 일찍 떠나**려고** 자기 전에 미리 가방을 준비해 두었다.
> I packed my bag before going to sleep in order to leave early tomorrow morning.

1 시에서 강조된 부분의 문법을 분석해 보세요. 어떤 단어와 문법이 쓰였습니까?

Look at the emphasized part of the poem and analyze its grammar. Which words and grammar were used?

$$\boxed{} = \boxed{} + \boxed{} \left(+ \boxed{} \right)$$

2 다음 표현을 써서 문장을 완성하세요.

Write out the following expressions and complete the sentences.

AV(으)려고

(가) 백설공주를 죽이다	① 서울로 유학을 떠났다.
(나) 토끼는 용왕을 속이다	② 세종은 한글을 만들었다.
(다) 혼자 한국어를 공부해 보다	③ 왕비는 독이 든 사과를 먹였다.
(라) 윤동주는 문학을 공부하다	④ 한강은 소설을 썼고 노벨 문학상을 받았다.
(마) 아픔을 겪은 사람들의 목소리를 전하다	⑤ 이 책을 사서 연습 중이다.
(바) 누구나 쉽게 글로 의사소통을 하게 하다	⑥ 바위 위에 긴을 꺼내 두고 왔다고 거짓말을 했다.

(가) 백설공주를 죽이려고 왕비는 독이 든 사과를 먹였다.

(나)

(다)

(라)

(마)

(바)

3 여러분은 문풍지가 무엇인지 알고 있나요? 문풍지에 구멍을 내어 밖을 엿보는 화자의 마음이 어땠을지 말해 봅시다.

Do you know what "문풍지" is? Describe what you think the speaker's feelings were when looking outside through the hole in the 문풍지.

43 츠르게네프의 언덕

나는 고갯길을 넘고 있었다 ······
그 때 세 소년 거지가 나를 지나쳤다.
첫째 아이는 잔등에 바구니를 둘러메고,
바구니 속에는 사이다 병, 통조림 통, 쇳조각,
헌 양말짝 등 폐품이 가득하였다.
둘째 아이도 그러하였다.
셋째 아이도 그러하였다.
텁수룩한 머리털, 시커먼 얼굴에 눈물 고인 충혈된 눈,
색 잃어 푸르스름한 입술, 너덜너덜한 누더기 옷, 찢겨진 맨발.
아 ── 얼마나 무서운 가난이 어 어린 소년들을 삼키었느냐!

나는 측은한 마음이 움직이었다.
나는 호주머니를 뒤지었다. 두툼한 지갑, 시계, 손수건 ······
있을 것은 죄다 있었다.
그러나 무턱대고 이것들을 내 줄 용기는 없었다.
손으로 만지작만지작거릴 뿐이었다.

다정스레 이야기나 하리라 하고 "얘들아" 불러보았다.
첫째 아이가 충혈된 눈으로 홀끔 돌려다 볼 뿐이었다.
둘째 아이도 그러할 뿐이었다.
셋째 아이도 그러할 뿐이었다.

그러고는 너는 상관없다는 듯이 자기네끼리
소근소근 이야기하면서 고개로 넘어갔다.

언덕 위에는 아무도 없었다.
짙어가는 황혼이 밀려들 뿐 ──

Turgenev's Hill

I was going over the hill road…… Then, three beggar boys passed me by.
The first child had a basket slung over his shoulder, and inside, the basket was
full up with junk: soda bottles, tinned food cans, pieces of scrap metal,
an old sock, and the like.
The second child, too, had the same.
The third child, too, had the same.
Shaggy hair, bloodshot eyes full of tears in sooty faces faces, bluish lips that had
lost their color, tattered rags for clothes, bare feet torn up.
Oh – What dreadful poverty had swallowed up these young boys!

My pitying heart was moved.
I turned out my pockets. Thick wallet, watch, handkerchief…… I had all of what
I needed.
But I lacked the courage to give them away. My hands simply fiddled with them.

Determined to have a friendly chat, I called out, "Hey, children!"
The first child simply turned his bloodshot eyes on me.
The second child, too, did only this.
The third child, too, did only this.

Then, whispering among themselves as if to say I had nothing to do with them,
they went over the hill.

There was nobody atop the hill then.
Only the darkening twilight flooding in –

Vocabulary

거지 beggar	시커멓다 to be dark	죄다 all, all together
지나치다 to pass by	고이다 to well up	무턱대고 thoughtless
잔등 back	충혈되다 to be bloodshot	만지작거리다 to fiddle with
둘러메다 to sling or carry over one's shoulder	푸르스름하다 to be bluish	흘끔 glance, looking at
	너덜너덜하다 to be in tatters	상관없다 to have nothing to do with
통조림 tinned food	누더기 rags	
쇳조각 scrap metal	찢겨지다 to be torn	소근소근 whisper
양말짝 pair of socks	가난 poverty	황혼 twilight
텁수룩하다 to be shaggy	뒤지다 to turn out	측은하다 to be pitiful
머리털 hair	두툼하다 to be thick	

N이나 AV

An auxiliary particle that indicates a choice that is made when you don't particularly like something, but have no other option. Like in "굿이나 보고 떡이나 먹자("Let's watch the shaman ritual and eat rice cake," with the meaning of "Sit back and enjoy the ride")," it is also used when choosing something that is the best, but pretending it isn't.

> (Ex) 그거**나** 가져라. Just take that one.
>
> 라면**이나** 끓여 먹자. Let's just cook and eat ramyeon.
>
> 할 일도 없는데 낮잠**이나** 자야겠다.
> I don't have anything to do, so I guess I'll have to take a nap.

1 시에서 강조된 부분의 문법을 분석해 보세요. 어떤 단어와 문법이 쓰였습니까?

Look at the emphasized part of the poem and analyze its grammar. Which words and grammar were used?

2 다음 표현을 써서 문장을 완성하세요.

Write out the following expressions and complete the sentences.

N(이)나 AV(으)ㄹ까/자

(가) 책을 읽다　　　　　　　➡ 책이나 읽을까?

(나) 빨래를 하다　　　　　　➡ ______________________________

(다) 컵라면을 먹다　　　　　➡ ______________________________

(라) 다시 잠을 자다　　　　➡ ______________________________

(마) 친구를 만나러 나가다　➡ ______________________________

(바) 태블릿으로 영화를 보다　➡ ______________________________

3 가난한 사람을 도운 적이 있나요? 도움이 필요한 아이들을 돕기 위해 어떤 제도가 필요한지 말해 봅시다.

Have you ever helped a poor person? Discuss what kind of systems are required to be in place to help children in need.

(44) 소년

여기저기서 단풍잎 같은 슬픈 가을이 뚝뚝 떨어진다. 단풍잎 떨어져 나온 자리마다 봄을 마련해 놓고 나뭇가지 위에 하늘이 펼쳐 있다. 가만히 하늘을 들여다보려면 눈썹에 파란 물감이 든다. 두 손으로 따뜻한 볼을 쓸어 보면 손바닥에도 파란 물감이 묻어난다. 다시 손바닥을 들여다본다. 손금에는 맑은 강물이 흐르고, 맑은 강물이 흐르고, 강물 속에는 사랑처럼 슬픈 얼굴 —— 아름다운 순이의 얼굴이 어린다. 소년은 황홀히 눈을 감아 본다. 그래도 맑은 강물은 흘러 사랑처럼 슬픈 얼굴 —— 아름다운 순이의 얼굴은 어린다.

MP3 44

The Boy

Here and there, the sorrowful autumn falls like autumn leaves, drop, drop. Each place from which the leaves fall prepares for the spring, and the sky is spread out above the tree branches. When he pauses to look into the sky, his eyebrows are tinted with blue. When he brushes his warm cheeks with two hands, his palms, too, are stained blue. He looks at his palms again. Along the creases, clear river water flows, clear river water flows, and in the river water, a face as sad as love – lovely Soon-yi's face is reflected back. The boy closes his eyes in rapture. And yet, the clear river water flows, and a face as sad as love – Only lovely Soon-yi's face shines back dimly.

Vocabulary

소년 boy
단풍잎 autumn leaves
뚝뚝 drip, drop
마련하다 to prepare
펼치다 to spread out
가만히 still, quietly
눈썹 eyebrow

물감 paint, dye
쓸다 to brush, to sweep
묻어나다 to stain, to smear
손바닥 palm
손금 the lines of one's palm
황홀히 ecstatically, in rapture

AV어/아 보다

An auxiliary verb that indicates the meaning of trying a certain action.

> (Ex) 옷은 입**어 보고** 사는 게 좋다. It's good to try on clothes when you buy them.
>
> 양쪽의 말을 다 들**어 봐야** 한다. You have to try listening to both sides of the story.
>
> 서울 여행을 한다면 인사동에는 꼭 한번 **가 볼** 만하다.
> If you travel to Seoul, it's definitely worth going to Insadong once.
>
> 쇼핑을 하고 나면 영수증에 적힌 내용을 꼼꼼히 따**져 본다.**
> After shopping, I carefully check over the things written on the receipt.

1 시에서 강조된 부분의 문법을 분석해 보세요. 어떤 단어와 문법이 쓰였습니까?
Look at the emphasized part of the poem and analyze its grammar. Which words and grammar were used?

	=		+			+	
	=		+		+		+	
	=		+			+	

2 다음 표현을 써서 문장을 완성하세요.
Write out the following expressions and complete the sentences.

어/아 보고	어/아 봐도	어/아 보자면서	어/아 봤지만	어/아 보면

신입생 환영회 때 처음 이야기를 (가) <u>나누어 보고</u> 순이에게 첫눈에 반했다.
　　　　　　　　　　　　　　　나누다

그래서 순이에게 한번 (나) ＿＿＿＿＿＿＿ 좋겠다고 고백을 했다.
　　　　　　　　　사귀다

순이는 아직 서로를 잘 모르니까 그냥 친구로 (다) ＿＿＿＿＿＿＿ 내 고백을 거절했다.
　　　　　　　　　　　　　　　　　　　지내다

순이에 대한 내 마음을 우정으로 바꾸려고 (라) ＿＿＿＿＿＿＿ 좋아하는 마음을
　　　　　　　　　　　　　　　　　노력하다

정리하기가 어렵다. 생각하지 않으려고 눈을 (마) ＿＿＿＿＿＿＿ 자꾸 순이 얼굴이 보인다.
　　　　　　　　　　　　　　　　감다

3 여러분은 사귀던 사람과 헤어져 본 경험이 있나요? 헤어지고 나서 그 사람을 잊기 위해 어떤 노력을 했는지 말해 봅시다.

Have you dated and then broken up with someone? Discuss what you did to try to forget that person after you broke up with them.

Vocabulary ____

첫눈에 반하다 to fall in love at first sight	감다 to close
고백 confession	헤어지다 to break up
거절하다 to turn down	잊다 to forget

(45) 위로

거미란 놈이 흉한 심보로 병원 뒤뜰 난간과 꽃밭 사이 사람 발이 잘 닿지 않는 곳에 그물을 쳐 놓았다. 옥외 요양을 받는 젊은 사나이가 누워서 쳐다보기 바르게 ——

나비가 한 마리 꽃밭에 날아 들다 그물에 걸리었다. 노 — 란 날개를 파득거려도 파득거려도 나비는 자꾸 감기우기만 한다. 거미가 쏜살같이 가더니 끝없는 끝없는 실을 뽑아 나비의 온몸을 감아 버린다. 사나이는 긴 한숨을 쉬었다.

나이보다 무수한 고생 끝에 때를 잃고 병을 얻은 이 사나이를 위로할 말이 —— 거미줄을 헝클어 버리는 것밖에 위로의 말이 없었다.

Comfort

A spider, in its ominous nature, cast its net in the backyard of the hospital, in the space between the railing and the flowerbed, where people's feet rarely touch. So that the young man lay convalescing outside could see it well from where he lay –

A butterfly flying into the flowerbed got caught in the net. Though it flaps and flaps its yellow, yellow wings, the butterfly only grows more entangled. Quick as an arrow, the spider approaches and winds the butterfly up whole in the endless, endless silk it pulls.
The man breathed a long sigh.

Some word to comfort the man who fell ill after hardships more numerous than due to his age –
There were no words of comfort, except for tangling up and sweeping the spiderweb away.

Vocabulary

위로 comfort	파득거리다 to flutter, to flap
거미 spider	감기다 to be wound up in
흉하다 to be ominous	쏜살같이 like an arrow (quickly)
심보 one's nature or temper	실 thread, silk
뒤뜰 backyard, back garden	뽑다 to pull, to draw
난간 railing	온몸 one's whole body
닿다 to touch, to reach	감다 to wind up
그물 net	한숨을 쉬다 to sigh, to breathe a sigh
옥외 outdoor	무수하다 numerous, countless
요양 convalescence, recovery	고생 hardship, suffering
날다 to fly	헝클다 to tangle up
걸리다 to get stuck, to get caught	

V1어/아도 V2기만 하다

-어/아도 is a connective ending that expresses a meaning of assumption or concession. It is used with -기만 하다 in the clause that follows, indicating that what unfolds in the clause that follows is contrary to the expectations derived from the situation preceding -어/아도. It is natural for the verb in the clause that follows to be an intransitive single word, and if the clause that follows includes a noun, it is natural for it to be changed to the form of N만 하다.

(Ex) 가진 게 없**어도** 마음은 편하**기만 하다**. My heart feels at ease even if I have nothing.

크게 성공하지 못**해도** 삶이 행복하**기만 하면** 된다.
Even if you can't succeed much, it's fine so long as your life is a happy one.

바람이 강하게 불어서 모자를 쓰고 장갑을 껴**도** 너무 춥다.
The wind is blowing so strongly that even if I wear a hat and gloves, it's too cold.

밤을 새우는 일이 있**어도** 내일까지는 보고서를 다 써야 한다.
Even if I stay up all night, I have to finish writing this whole report by tomorrow.

---

1 시에서 강조된 부분의 문법을 분석해 보세요. 어떤 단어와 문법이 쓰였습니까?

Look at the emphasized part of the poem and analyze its grammar. Which words and grammar were used?

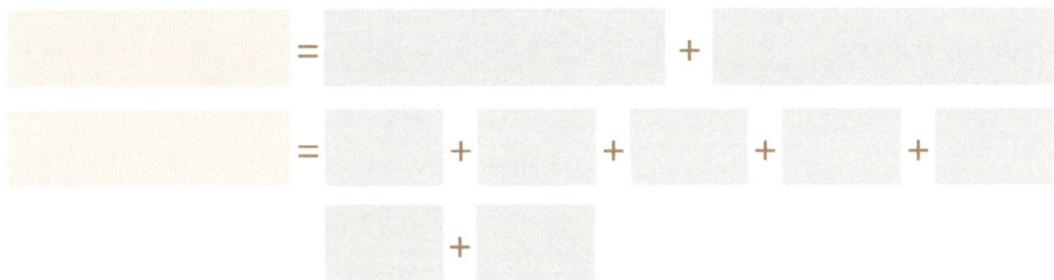

2 다음 표현을 써서 문장을 완성하세요.

Write out the following expressions and complete the sentences.

V1어/아도 V2기만 했다.

(가) <u>바람이 불어도 덥기만 한</u> 여름에 아들 청개구리와 엄마 청개구리가 살고 있었습니다.
     (바람이 불다 / 덥다)

엄마 청개구리는 건강이 점점 안 좋아져서 (나) ________________________________.
                                          (약을 먹다 / 나빠지다)

아들 청개구리가 학교에 가고 나서 오전 내내 (다) ________________________________.
                                          (쉬다 / 피곤하다)

(라) ____. 아들 개구리는 엄마가 심한 병에 걸린 것을
(방 온도를 높이다 / 춥다)

모르고 엄마 말을 하나도 듣지 않았습니다. 아들은 엄마가 (마) ____________________________.
(열심히 공부하라도 하다 / 놀다)

집에 돌아오면 (바) ____________________________________.
(손부터 씻으라고 하다 / 그냥 먹다)

엄마 개구리는 죽은 뒤에 산에 묻히고 싶었습니다.
그런데 아들 개구리가 늘 반대로만 하니까
자기가 죽으면 강가가 묻으라는 말을 남기고
죽었습니다. 하지만 엄마가 죽고 나서야
정신을 차려야겠다고 생각한 아들 개구리는
돌아가신 엄마를 강가에 묻었습니다.
그 후로 아들 개구리는 비만 오면 엄마의 무덤이
떠내려갈까 계속 슬프게 울었습니다.

3 거미줄을 끊어서 나비를 구해 주는 것을 보고 이 시에 나오는 '아픈 사나이'는 위로를 받았을
까요? 이 사람을 어떻게 위로할 수 있을지 말해 봅시다.

Do you think the "sick man" in the poem was comforted by seeing the spiderweb broken
off and the butterfly saved? Discuss how you would comfort this person.

201

(46) 병원

살구나무 그늘로 얼굴을 가리고, 병원 뒤뜰에 누워, 젊은 여자가 흰옷 아래로 하얀 다리를 드러내 놓고 일광욕을 한다. 한나절이 기울도록 가슴을 앓는다는 이 여자를 찾아오는 이, 나비 한 마리도 없다. 슬프지도 않은 살구나무 가지에는 바람조차 없다.

나도 모를 아픔을 오래 참다 처음으로 이곳에 찾아왔다. 그러나 나의 늙은 의사는 젊은이의 병을 모른다. 나한테는 병이 없다고 한다. 이 지나친 시련, 이 지나친 피로, 나는 성내서는 안 된다.

여자는 자리에서 일어나 옷깃을 여미고 화단에서 금잔화 한 포기를 따 가슴에 꽂고 병실 안으로 사라진다. 나는 그 여자의 건강이 —— 아니 내 건강도 속히 회복되기를 바라며 그가 누웠던 자리에 누워 본다.

Background Knowledge

During the time when Yoon Dong-ju was attending Yonhi College (Chosen Christian College), Korea's first Western-style hospital was Gwanghyewon (founded in 1885), which would become today's Severance Hospital. Seeing the patients of this hospital, which was located within the Yonhi College campus, Yoon Dong-ju sympathized greatly with their suffering. It's even said that he considered naming a collection of his poems "Hospital," because at the time, he thought the entire Korean Peninsula was full of people who were sick. In 1940, when this poem was written, Jeong Byeong-uk entered Yonhi College, and began a friendship with Yoon Dong-ju, who had entered in 1938. In this year, Yoon Dong-ju took an English Bible class while attending Hyeopseong Church, and learned the Book of Odes from the teacher, his maternal uncle, Kim Yak-yeon.

Hospital

Hiding her face in the shade of an apricot tree, laying in the yard of the hospital, a young woman sunbathes, sticking white legs out from under white clothing. Even after most of the day has passed, the young woman, who they say has a weak heart, is sought out by no one, not even a single butterfly. There is not even a breeze in the branches of the apricot tree, which feels no sadness.

I, too, who withstood my pain for so long without knowing, have come to this place for the first time. But my old doctor doesn't know this young man's disease. He says I have no illness. This overwhelming torment, this overwhelming fatigue; but I must not get angry.

The woman stands up from her place, straightens her clothing, picks a marigold from the flowerbed, pins it to her breast, and disappears inside her hospital room. Wishing for the woman's health – no, for my own health, as well, to quickly recover, I lie down in the place where she lay.

Vocabulary

살구나무 apricot tree	성(을) 내다 to get angry
그늘 shade	자리 place, seat
눕다 to lie down	옷깃 collar, clothing
젊다 to be young	여미다 to adjust
하얗다 to be white	화단 flowerbed
일광욕 sunbath	금잔화 marigold
한나절 half a day, most of a day	꽂다 to pin
기울다 to wane, to pass by	병실 hospital room
앓다 to be ill, to be sick	사라지다 to disappear
지나치다 to be overwhelming, to be excessive	속히 quick, soon
시련 ordeal, hardship, suffering	회복되다 to get better, to be recovered

V도록

A connective ending that expresses that the content of the preceding clause becomes the purpose, result, method, or degree of the clause that follows. When used with expressions indicating time, it takes on the meaning of emphasizing the passage of time. It is used to emphasize that a negative psychological effect occurs, such as worry, disappointment, or frustration, when a predetermined party doesn't accomplish something that needs to be done by a certain set time.

Ex 학생들은 밤이 새**도록** 토론을 했다. The students debated all night long.

아빠가 편히 주무시**도록** 조용히 하자. Let's be quiet so that Dad can sleep comfortably.

아무리 대학생이 되었다고 해도 자녀가 12시가 넘**도록** 집에 돌아오지 않으면 부모는 걱정이 된다. Even if their child has become a college student, if they don't come home by after 12 o'clock, parents will worry.

학교 앞 횡단보도 근처에서 운전을 할 때는 아이들이 길을 안전하게 건너**도록** 특히 더 주의해야 한다. When driving near the crosswalk in front of a school, you must take special care so that children can cross the street safely.

1 시에서 강조된 부분의 문법을 분석해 보세요. 어떤 단어와 문법이 쓰였습니까?

Look at the emphasized part of the poem and analyze its grammar. Which words and grammar were used?

	=		+	

2 관계있는 것을 연결한 뒤 다음 표현을 써서 문장을 완성하세요.

Connect the items that are related, then write out the following expressions and complete the sentences.

V도록

(가) 낮 두 시가 넘다 •   • ① 늦잠을 잤다.

(나) 이 나이가 되다 •   • ② 배달 음식이 안 온다.

(다) 한 시간이 지나다 •   • ③ 점심을 못 먹었다.

(라) 수도관이 얼지 않다 •   • ④ 추가 설명을 제시하였다.

(마) 해가 하늘 중천에 뜨다 •   • ⑤ 겨울에는 야외 공원의 샤워장을 잠가 둔다.

(바) 시를 잘 이해하다 •   • ⑥ 외국어 하나 제대로 못 배운 것이 후회가 된다.

(가) 낮 두 시가 넘도록 점심을 못 먹었다.

(나) ____

(다) ____

(라) ____

(마) ____

(바) ____

3 누구를 만나러 병원에 간 적이 있나요? 그 사람에게 어떤 말로 위로를 전했어요? 병문안을 간 경험에 대해 말해 봅시다.

Have you ever gone to the hospital to meet someone? What did you say to that person to comfort them? Discuss what your visit was like.

⑰ 무서운 시간

거 나를 부르는 것이 누구요

가랑잎 이파리 푸르러 나오는 그늘인데
나 아직 여기 호흡이 남아 있소.

한 번도 손들어 보지 못한 나를
손들어 표할 하늘도 없는 나를

어디에 내 한 몸 둘 하늘이 있어
나를 부르는 것이오.

일을 마치고 내 죽는 날 아침에는
서럽지도 않은 가랑잎이 떨어질 텐데……

나를 부르지 마오.

MP3 47

A Frightening Time

Who are you that calls me, there?

In the shade where fallen leaves turn green,
I, here, still draw breath.

I, who have not once raised my hand,
I, who have no heaven to raise my hand to point to,

Somewhere, there's a heaven in which to place my body,
That is calling out to me.

On the morning of the day I die, after I have finished my work,
The leaves will fall without sorrow……

Do not call for me.

Vocabulary

가랑잎 fallen leaf, dead leaf	호흡 breath
이파리 leaf	남다 to remain
푸르다 to be green, to be blue	표하다 to point out

1 시에서 강조된 부분의 문법을 분석해 보세요. 어떤 단어와 문법이 쓰였습니까?

Look at the emphasized part of the poem and analyze its grammar. Which words and grammar were used?

2 관계있는 것을 연결한 뒤 다음 표현을 써서 문장을 완성하세요.

Connect the items that are related, then write out the following expressions and complete the sentences.

V(으)ㄹ 텐데

(가) 뒤에서 따라오기 힘들다	① 좀 천천히 걷자.
(나) 미세 먼지가 건강에 안 좋다	② 자주 연락드리겠습니다.
(다) 출근 시간이라서 차가 밀리다	③ 30분 일찍 출발해야겠다.
(라) 제가 떠나면 많이 섭섭하시다	④ 오다가다 종종 들르세요.
(마) 오래 앉아 있으면 허리가 아프다	⑤ 가끔 스트레칭이라도 해라.
(바) 이사 와서 아는 사람도 많이 없다	⑥ 외출할 때는 항상 마스크를 챙기세요.

(가) 뒤에서 따라오기 힘들 텐데 좀 천천히 걷자.

(나) ____

(다) ____

(라) ____

(마) ____

(바) ____

3 지금 마음속에 걱정이 있나요? 어떤 걱정인지 말해 봅시다.

Do you have any worries right now? Discuss what kind of worries you have.

Vocabulary

시장하다 to be hungry   오다가다 to come around

섭섭하다 to be disappointed, to be sorry   종종 now and then, sometimes

(48) 쉽게 씌어진 시

창밖에 밤비가 속살거려
육첩방은 남의 나라.

시인이란 슬픈 천명인 줄 알면서도
한 줄 시를 적어볼까.

땀내와 사랑내 포근히 품긴
보내주신 학비 봉투를 받아

대학 노 ― 트를 끼고
늙은 교수의 강의 들으러 간다.

생각해 보면 어린 때 동무를
하나, 둘, 죄다 잃어버리고

나는 무얼 바라
나는 다만, 홀로 침전하는 것일까?
인생은 살기 어렵다는데
시가 이렇게 쉽게 씌어지는 것은
부끄러운 일이다.

육첩방은 남의 나라
창밖에 밤비가 속살거리는데

등불을 밝혀 어둠을 조금 내몰고
시대처럼 올 아침을 기다리는 최후의 나.

나는 나에게 작은 손을 내밀어
눈물과 위안으로 잡는 최초의 악수.

Background Knowledge From April to June of 1942, when Yoon Dong-ju was studying abroad at Rikkyo University, he sent 5 poems including *A Poem Easily Written* to his friend Kang Cheo-joong in Seoul. These poems are the last that we can today confirm to be his. A year after this, in July 1943, Yoon Dong-ju was arrested along with Song Mong-gyu and others by the Japanese police.

A Poem Easily Written

The night rain whispers outside the window
Of the six-mat wide room in this strange land.

Knowing full well that a poet's destiny is a sad one,
Shall I write a line of poetry?

Having received the envelope of tuition money,
Full up with the comfortable smell of sweat and the smell of love,

With a college notebook tucked under my arm,
I go off to attend an old professor's lecture.

When I think about it, my childhood friends
Have been lost, one, two... all of them.

What do I wish for
As I, alone, sink down by myself?
They say that living life is hard,
And it's shameful, then, that a poem can be written so easily.

The six-mat wide room in a strange land,
The night rain whispers outside the window,

And I light the lamp to drive the darkness out a little,
And in my last moments, I wait for the morning that will come on
like an age.

I extend a small hand to myself
And grab it in the first handshake, with tears and comfort.

Vocabulary

속살거리다 to whisper	홀로 alone
육(6)첩방 a 6-cheop room (a room 6 tatami mats wide)	침전하다 to sink into, to fall
남 stranger	인생 life
천명 destiny, life	등불 lamp
땀내 the smell of sweat	내몰다 to push back, to drive out
포근히 comfortably, snugly	최후 last
품기다 to be full with	위안 comfort
학비 tuition fees	최초 first
봉투 envelope	

V는/은 줄 알면서도

줄 is a dependent noun with the meaning of a certain method or judgment. It is used with 알다 and 모르다 to indicate the degree of the speaker's background knowledge. -면서도, which is the form of -면서 with 도 added, expresses that the clause that follows contains an action that contrasts with the content of the preceding clause.

> **Ex** 그가 나를 속일 **줄은** 꿈에도 생각하지 못했다. I couldn't even dream that he would trick me.
>
> 날마다 연습해야 하**는 줄 알면서도** 바쁘니까 자꾸 안 하게 된다.
> Even knowing that I need to practice every day, I'm busy, so I often am unable to.
>
> 그가 공부를 잘하**는 줄은 알았지만** 전체에서 일 등인 줄은 몰랐다.
> I knew that he was good at studying, but I didn't know that he was in first place.
>
> 거짓말을 하면 안 되**는 줄 알면서도** 할아버지 앞에서는 사실 대로 말할 수가 없었다.
> Even knowing that I shouldn't lie, I couldn't tell the truth in front of my grandfather.

1 시에서 강조된 부분의 문법을 분석해 보세요. 어떤 단어와 문법이 쓰였습니까?

Look at the emphasized part of the poem and analyze its grammar. Which words and grammar were used?

	=		+		+	
		+			+	

2 관계있는 것을 연결한 뒤 다음 표현을 써서 문장을 완성하세요.

Connect the items that are related, then write out the following expressions and complete the sentences.

V는/은 줄 알면서도

(가) 당분이 몸에 안 좋다	① 생각할수록 기분이 나쁘다.
(나) 내 체력으로 무리이다	② 할머니를 속일 수밖에 없었다.
(다) 친구의 말이 농담이다	③ 아이가 원하는 유학을 허락했다.
(라) 거짓말을 하면 안 되다	④ 산 정상까지 오를 계획을 세웠다.
(마) 이맘때 엄마 생신이 있다	⑤ 서너 시가 되면 자꾸 단 걸 찾는다.
(바) 떠나보내고 나서 후회하다	⑥ 회사 일이 바빠서 잊고 말았다.

(가)

(나) ____

(다) ____

(라) ____

(마) ____

(바) ____

3 결과가 좋지 않을 줄 알면서도 한 일이 있나요? 왜 미리 대비하지 못했는지 말해 봅시다.

Have you ever done something even though you knew the result wouldn't be good? Discuss why you couldn't prepare in advance.

Vocabulary

당분 sugar	속이다 to cheat, to deceive
무리 impossible	유학 study abroad
농담 joke	허락 permission
거짓말 lie	정상 summit
이맘때 at about this time	음력 lunar calendar

（49） 참회록

파란 녹이 낀 구리 거울 속에
내 얼굴이 남아 있는 것은
어느 왕조의 유물이기에
이다지도 욕될까.

나는 나의 참회의 글을 한 줄에 줄이자.
―― 만 이십사 년 일 개월을
무슨 기쁨을 바라 살아왔던가.

내일이나 모레나 그 어느 즐거운 날에
나는 또 한 줄의 참회록을 써야 한다.
―― 그때 그 젊은 나이에
왜 그런 부끄런 고백을 했던가.

밤이면 밤마다 나의 거울을
손바닥으로 발바닥으로 닦아 보자.

그러면 어느 운석 밑으로 홀로 걸어가는
슬픈 사람의 뒷모양이
거울 속에 나타나온다.

Background Knowledge This poem was written five days before Yoon Dong-ju changed his name to "Hiranuma Douju" in a process called 창씨개명(Changssi Gaemyeong). This poem is about shame, reflection, and introspection on the part of a people who have lost their country. His name change was required to complete documents for his study abroad in Japan.

MP3 49

Confession

In the copper mirror tinged with green rust
My face remains.
Which dynasty's legacy is it
That gives me this much shame?

Let me condense my confession into a single line.
— For 24 years and one month,
What joy have I longed for that has kept me alive?

Tomorrow or the day after, on that joyful day,
I must write another line of confession.
— Back then, in my youth,
Why did I make such a shameful admission?

Night after night, I shall
Wipe my mirror with the palms of my hands and the soles of my feet.

And then, under a shooting star, walking alone,
The figure of a sad man seen from behind
Appears in the mirror.

Vocabulary ____

참회록 confession
파랗다 to be blue
녹 rust
끼다 to lace, to tinge, to tint
구리 copper

왕조 dynasty
유물 artifact, relic, legacy
욕되다 to be shameful, to be disgraced
만 indicator of international age
운석 shooting star, meteorite

이면 is a conjunctive particle that connects two or more things based on similar qualifications. Two or more noun phrases with the same noun or similar category of nouns are connected before and after this particle, and if used with the auxiliary particle 마다, meaning "each and every," the meaning expressed is "all (of that noun or noun phrase)." As it repeats the same noun, it can also emphasize a positive or negative feeling.

> **Ex** 밤**이면** 밤**마다** 달을 보면서 소원을 빌었다. I made a wish on the moon each and every night.
>
> 우리 엄마는 날**이면** 날**마다** 잔소리를 한다. My mother nags me each and every day.
>
> 요즘 연예인은 노래**면** 노래, 연기**면** 연기, 못 하는 게 없다.
> Celebrities these days sing when it comes to singing, and act when it comes to acting – there's nothing they can't do.
>
> 고마우신 선생님께 명절**이면** 명절**마다** 선물을 보내고 있다.
> Each and every holiday, I send a gift to my teacher to whom I'm thankful.
>
> 옆에 앉은 친구가 쉬는 시간**이면** 쉬는 시간**마다** 엎드려 잔다.
> Each and every rest period, the friend who sits next to me lies down and sleeps.

1 시에서 강조된 부분의 문법을 분석해 보세요. 어떤 단어와 문법이 쓰였습니까?

Look at the emphasized part of the poem and analyze its grammar. Which words and grammar were used?

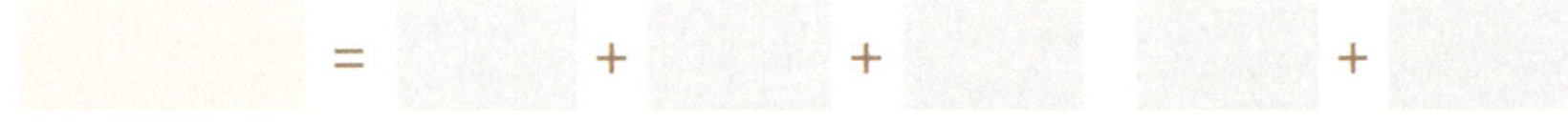

2 관계있는 것을 연결한 뒤 다음 표현을 써서 문장을 완성하세요.

Connect the items that are related, then write out the following expressions and complete the sentences.

N이면 N마다

(가) 벽	① 투숙객이 가득해 만원이었다.
(나) 방	② 아이의 이름표가 붙어 있었다.
(다) 봄	③ 베란다의 군자란이 꽃을 피운다.
(라) 밤	④ 달님을 보며 고향집을 떠올렸다.
(마) 가방	⑤ 연예인 얼굴로 도배가 돼 있었다.

(가) 벽이면 벽마다 연예인 얼굴로 도배가 돼 있었다.

(나) ____________________________________

(다) ____________________________________

(라) ____________________________________

(마) ____________________________________

3 <참회록>에서 희로애락(기쁨, 노여움, 슬픔, 즐거움)의 감정 중 어떤 감정이 어떤 단어로
표현되었나요? 또 단어로 표현되지는 않았지만 문장에 숨어 있는 감정은 어떤 게 있는지
말해 봅시다.

In "Confession," which emotions (out of joy, anger, sadness, and pleasure) were conveyed
with which words? Also discuss which emotions were not expressed in words but are
hidden in the sentences.

군자란*

Vocabulary

투숙객 guest	안부 greetings, one's well-being
만원 full, a full house	노여움 anger
이름표 name tag	감정 emotion
*군자란 Kafir lily	표현 expression
연예인 celebrity	숨다 to hide
도배 wallpaper	

(50) 별 헤는 밤

계절이 지나가는 하늘에는
가을로 가득 차 있습니다.

나는 아무 걱정도 없이
가을 속의 별들을 다 헤일 듯합니다.

가슴 속에 하나 둘 새겨지는 별을
이제 다 못 헤는 것은
쉬이 아침이 오는 까닭이요,
내일 밤이 남은 까닭이요,
아직 나의 청춘이 다하지 않은 까닭입니다.

별 하나에 추억과
별 하나에 사랑과
별 하나에 쓸쓸함과
별 하나에 동경과
별 하나에 시와
별 하나에 어머니, 어머니,

어머님, 나는 별 하나에 아름다운 말 한마디씩 불러봅니다. 소학교 때 책상을 같이했던 아이들의 이름과, 패, 경, 옥 이런 이국 소녀들의 이름과 벌써 애기 어머니 된 계집애들의 이름과, 가난한 이웃 사람들의 이름과, 비둘기, 강아지, 토끼, 노새, 노루, "프란시스 잠", "라이너 마리아 릴케" 이런 시인의 이름을 불러봅니다.

이네들은 너무나 멀리 있습니다.
별이 아슬히 멀 듯이,

어머님,
그리고 당신은 멀리 북간도에 계십니다.

나는 무엇인지 그리워
이 많은 별빛이 내린 언덕 위에
내 이름자를 써보고,
흙으로 덮어 버리었습니다.

딴은 밤을 새워 우는 벌레는
부끄러운 이름을 슬퍼하는 까닭입니다.

그러나 겨울이 지나고 나의 별에도 봄이 오면
무덤 위에 파란 잔디가 피어나듯이
내 이름자 묻힌 언덕 위에도
자랑처럼 풀이 무성할 게외다.

Background Knowledge

In December 1941, following the shortening of the school semester due to the war, Yoon Dong-ju graduated from Yonhi College(Chosen Christian College) 3 months earlier than expected. Then, in the spring of 1942, before leaving to study abroad in Japan, he tried to publish a collection of poems called *Sky, Wind, Stars and Poems*, but couldn't accomplish this because he was short of money. He made 3 copies of his handwritten manuscript, and kept one for himself; gave one to his teacher, Lee Yang Ha; and one to his junior, Jeong Byeong-uk. In January 1944, Jeong Byeong-uk entrusted his copy to his mother in Gwangyang, South Jeollado Province, saying, "This is as precious as a life, so please keep it safe." In 1946, the manuscript Jeong Byeong-uk had left was published as *Sky, Wind, Stars and Poems*.

A Night Counting Stars

The sky in which the seasons pass
Is full up with autumn.

I feel as if I can count all of the stars in autumn
Without any trouble at all.

One by one, the stars carved into my heart
The reason that I cannot yet count,
Is that morning comes soon —
Is that tomorrow night remains —
Is that my youth is not yet spent.

One star is memory,
And one star is love,
And one star is loneliness,
And one star is yearning,
And one star is poetry,
And one star is mother, mother,

Mother, I try to name each one of the stars with a beautiful word. The
names of the children who shared a desk with me in elementary school; the
names of the foreign girls like Pae, Kyung, Ok; the names of the girls who
have already become mothers; the names of our impoverished neighbors;
dove, puppy, rabbit, mule, and deer; the names of poets like Francis Jammes
and Rainer Maria Rilke.

All of them are much too far off.
Far off like the distant stars,

Mother,
And you are far off in North Gando.

Longing for something,
I wrote my name down
On the hill where all this starlight fell,
And covered it over with dirt.

Maybe the insects that sing throughout the night
Might pity shameful names.

But when winter passes and spring comes to my star as well,
Like the grass blooming over a grave,
On the hill where my name is buried,
Greenery will grow full and proud.

Vocabulary

헤다 to count
새기다 to carve, to engrave
까닭 reason
청춘 youth
다하다 to run out, to be exhausted
쓸쓸함 loneliness
동경 yearning
소학교 elementary school
계집 girl, woman

이네 them, these people
아슬하다 very far or high
별빛 starlight
딴 perhaps, well, that is to say
무덤 grave, tomb
잔디 grass
묻히다 to be buried
무성하다 to be thick, to be full

DV이/히

An affix that is added to an adjective stem to turn the adjective into an adverb. 이 is usually added after nouns or irregular ㅂ verbs. In the case of words made with 하다, 히 is usually added, but exceptionally, if the final consonant of the root word is ㅅ or ㄱ, then 이 is added. It is natural to use an adverb right before the verb that it modifies.

Ex 솔직**히** honestly   깊숙**이** deeply   끔찍**이** horribly

집집**이** from door to door   틈틈**이** in spare time   나날**이** day by day

조용**히** quietly   다행**히** luckily   무사**히** safely

1 시에서 강조된 부분의 문법을 분석해 보세요. 어떤 단어와 문법이 쓰였습니까?

Look at the emphasized part of the poem and analyze its grammar. Which words and grammar were used?

2 관계있는 것을 연결한 뒤 다음 표현을 써서 문장을 완성하세요.

Connect the items that are related, then write out the following expressions and complete the sentences.

DV이/히

(가) 친구는 꼼꼼하다	① 꽃피어 있는 관광지이다.
(나) 지하철은 분주하다	② 누워서 천장을 올려다 보았다.
(다) 줄리엣은 반듯하다	③ 닦아서 선반 위에 올려 두어라.
(라) 네가 마신 물컵은 깨끗하다	④ 출근하는 사람들로 만원이었다.
(마) 경주는 불교문화가 찬란하다	⑤ 내 손을 잡으며 안부를 물으셨다.
(바) 이모는 따뜻하다	⑥ 원룸 계약서를 읽었다.

(가) 친구는 꼼꼼히 원룸 계약서를 읽었다.
____

(나) ____

(다) ____

(라) ____

(마) ____

(바) ____

3 밤하늘의 별이 몇 개인지 세어 본 적이 있어요? 그 별들에 좋은 말이나 이름을 하나씩 붙여 봅시다.

Have you ever counted how many stars were in the night sky? Give good words or names to each of those stars.

Vocabulary ____

꼼꼼하다 to be meticulous

분주하다 to be busy

반듯하다 to be straight; to be smooth

찬란하다 to be splendid; to be brilliant

선반 shelf

천장 ceiling

계약서 contract

부록

모범 답안 Model Answer

문법·해설 번역 Grammar & Explanation Translations

색인 Index

01 봄 1 Spring 1

1 나뭇가지에 = 나무 + ㅅ + 가지 + 에
한가운데서 = 한 * + 가운데 + 에서

2 (나) ②　　　　(다) ①
(라) ⑤　　　　(마) ④

02 못 자는 밤 Sleepless Nights

1 하나 , 둘 , 셋 , 넷
많기도 = 많 + 기 + 도

2 DV기도 하다

(나) ②, 아이가 정말 귀엽기도 하네요. /
예쁘기도 하다.
(다) ①, 오늘 날씨가 참 덥기도 하다. /
춥기도 하네요.

Adv도 V

(라) ⑥, 한 통, 두 통, 세 통, … 메일함에
메일이 참 많이도 쌓였다.
(마) ④, 한 시간, 두 시간, 세 시간, … 게임을 참
오래도 한다.
(바) ⑤, 열 명, 스무 명, 서른 명, … 공연장 입구에
사람이 참 빨리도 는다.

03 무얼 먹고 사나
What Do They Live Off Of?

1 무얼 = 무엇 + 을

2 (나) 누구, 누굴　　(다) 나, 날
(라) 무엇, 뭘　　(마) 그것, 그걸
(바) 어디, 어딜　　(사) 너, 널

04 나무 Tree

1 추면 = 추 + 면
잠잠하면 = 잠잠하 + 면

2 (나) 꽃이 피면 아가씨가 오고 꽃이 지면 아가씨도
갑니다.
(다) 아가씨가 오면 꽃이 피고 아가씨가 가면 꽃도
집니다.
(라) 비가 오면 고양이가 숨고 눈이 오면 산새가
숨습니다.
(마) 고양이가 숨으면 비가 오고 산새가 숨으면
눈이 옵니다.
(바) 나뭇가지에 해가 걸리면 낮이 되고 나뭇가지
에 달이 걸리면 밤이 됩니다.

05 산울림 Echo

1 못 들은 = 못 들 + 은
들었다 = 들 + 었 + 다 *

2 (나) 매운 음식을 잘 못 먹어요.
매운 음식을 잘 먹지 못해요.
(다) 요즘 밤에 잠을 잘 못 자요.
·요즘 밤에 잠을 잘 자지 못해요.
(라) 한국어를 그렇게 잘 못해요.
한국어를 그렇게 잘 하지 못해요.

06 식권 Meal Ticket

1 물로 = 물 + 로
쌀로 = 쌀 + 로

2 (나) 이천 쌀로 지은 밥이 맛있다.
(다) 밀양 사과로 만든 사과 주스를 마셔 볼래?
(라) 순창 고추장으로 끓인 찌개 맛이 기가 막히다.
(마) 강원도 감자로 만든 감자떡이 달고 맛있다.
(바) 에티오피아 커피로 만든 바닐라 라떼가 참
고소하다.

07 병아리 Chicks

1 쥐 = 주 + 어

  기다려 = 기다려 + 어

2 (나) 개 / 멍멍 / ⑤
   소가 음매 하며 풀을 뜯고 있어.
 (다) 까치 / 깍깍 / ④
   까치가 깍깍 하며 한 나무 위로 모였어.
 (라) 참새 / 짹짹 / ⑥
   참새가 짹짹 하며 창문 밖에서 아침
   인사를 해.
 (마) 고양이 / 야옹 / ③
   고양이가 야옹 하며 책장 위로 올라갔어.
 (바) 호랑이 / 어흥 / ②
   호랑이가 어흥 하며 토끼를 따라갔어.

08 가슴 3 Heart 3

1 도는 = 돌 + 는

  떤다 = 떨 + 는

2 (나) 제가 만든 케이크인데 맛이 어때요?
 (다) 긴 머리보다 짧은 머리가 더 편해요.
 (라) 저와 누나는 서울에 살고 부모님은 부산에
   사십니다.
 (마) 제가 사는 원룸은 학교에서 좀 멀지만 방도
   크고 값도 싸요.

Grammar Tip

	-고	-은/ㄴ	-(으)ㄹ	-(스)ㅂ니다
살다	살고	산	살	삽니다
알다	알고	안	알	압니다
팔다	팔고	판	팔	팝니다
열다	열고	연	열	엽니다
놀다	놀고	논	놀	놉니다
만들다	만들고	만든	만들	만듭니다
길다	길고	긴	길	깁니다
멀다	멀고	먼	멀	멉니다

09 할아버지 Grandfather

1 달다고 하오 = 달 + 다 + 고
     하 + 오

2 (나) 떡 본 김에 제사 지내자고 합니다.
 (다) 그 정도는 누워서 떡 먹기라고 합니다.
 (라) 남의 떡이 더 커 보이는 법이라고 합니다.
 (마) 한국 속담에는 왜 떡이 많이 나오냐고 합니다.
 (바) 떡 줄 사람은 생각도 않는데 김칫국부터
   마시지 말라고 합니다.

10 호주머니 Pockets

1 겨울만 되면 = 겨울 + 만 되 + 면

2 (나) 책만 펴면 잠이 쏟아진다.
 (다) 봄만 되면 한국은 황사가 심해진다.
 (라) 친구와 약속만 잡으면 회사에 일이 생긴다
 (마) 5시 50분만 되면 퇴근 준비를 한다.

11 개 1 Dog 1

1 눈 위에서 = 눈 위 + 에서

2 (나) 사과 (다) 눈
 (라) 벌 (마) 말

12 오줌싸개 지도
Map of the Bedwetter

1 지돈가 = 지도 + 인가

2 (나) 명동역은 3호선인가 4호선인가?
 (다) 여기(이태원)는 한국인가 외국인가?
 (라) 커피는 건강에 이로운가 해로운가?
 (마) 약속 장소는 고속터미널 역에서 가까운가
   먼가?
 (바) 한국대학교의 입학식 날짜는 3월 1일인가
   3월 2일인가?

13 이불 Blanket

1 지붕이랑 = 지붕 + 이랑

길이랑 = 길 + 이랑

밭이랑 = 밭 + 이랑

2 (나) 비가 오네요. 산이랑 공원이랑 목말라한다고
뿌려 주는 물인가 봐.

(다) 구름이 끼네요. 새랑 나무가 뜨겁다고
발라 주는 선크림인가 봐.

(라) 달이 밝네요. 너랑 나랑 밤길이 무섭다고
켜 주는 가로등인가 봐.

(마) 해가 나네요. 강과 바다가 우울해한다고
위로해 주는 손길인가 봐.

14 그 여자 That Woman

1 집어 갔습니 = 집 + 어 (가지고)

가 + 았 + 습니다

2 (나) 선물을 하나씩 준비해 가지고 오세요.

(다) 시간이 늦어 가지고 연락을 못 드렸어요.

(라) 점심을 많이 먹어 가지고 저녁을 못 먹겠다.

(마) 소설을 한 편 써 가지고 책으로 내고 싶다.

(바) 한국말을 배워 가지고 자막 없이 드라마를
보면 좋겠다.

15 해바라기 얼굴 Sunflower-like Face

1 뜨자 = 뜨 + 자

2 (나) 우산을 사자 비가 그쳤다.

(다) 침대에 눕자 잠이 들었다.

(라) 해가 지자 기온이 뚝 떨어졌다.

(마) 유튜브 앱을 열자 추천 동영상이 떴다.

16 가슴 2 Heart 2

1 웃음 웃는 = 웃 + 음 웃 + 는

2 (나) 유학 생활을 재미있게 즐기기 바란다.

(다) 한국어로 팬레터를 쓰는 것이 내 꿈이다.

(라) 여행을 가기 위해서 한국말을 공부한다.

(마) 밤에 게임을 안 하기로 마음먹기가 쉽지
않다.

(바) 요즘 할 일이 많기 때문에 시간을 내기가
좀 어렵다.

17 반딧불 Fireflies

1 주우러 = 줍 + 으러

가자 = 가 + 자

2 (나) 시험 공부를 하러 카페로 가자.

(다) 눈사람을 만들러 운동장으로 나가자.

(라) 벚꽃 사진을 찍으러 여의도로 가자.

(마) 단풍 구경을 하러 설악산으로 가자.

18 산협의 오후
Mountain Valley Afternoon

1 슬프구나 = 슬프 + 구나

졸려 = 졸리 + 어

2 (나) 윤동주가 사용한 시어는 참 아름답다.

(다) 윤동주의 다른 시들도 검색해 봐라.

(라) '산협'과 같은 뜻을 가진 단어를 찾아보자.

(마) 한글 시를 이해하려면 한자도 좀
알아야 되는구나.

(바) 이 시 말고 다른 한글 시를 읽어 본 적이
있니?

19 고향집 — 만주에서 부른
My Home — Called for from Manchuria

1 끄을고 = 끌 + 고

건너서 = 건너 + 어서

2 (나) 카페에 들러서 커피를 사 가지고 수업에
간다.

(다) 오늘 아침에 일어나서 간밤 뉴스부터
확인했다.

(라) 한복을 입고 경복궁에 가면 무료로 입장할 수
있다.

(마) 친구를 만나서 같이 고속버스 터미널에
가려고 한다.

(바) 감기가 유행할 때는 마스크를 끼고 버스를
　　타는 게 좋다.

20　새로운 길　A New Path

1　숲으로 = 숲 + 으로

　　마을로 = 마을 + 로

2　(나) 어디로 가야 할지 모르겠다.

　　(다) 기사님, 서울역으로 가 주세요.

　　(라) 하늘로 솟았나, 땅속으로 꺼졌나.

　　(마) 오른쪽으로 쭉 가시면 공원이 나올 거예요.

　　(바) 꼭대기 층으로 올라가시면 전망이 더
　　　　좋습니다.

21　귀뚜라미와 나와
The Cricket and I

1　주지 말고 = 주 + 지　말 + 고

　　알자고 약속했다 = 알 + 자 + 고

　　　　　　　　　약속하 + 였 + 다

2　(나) ②　　　　　(다) ①
　　(라) ⑤　　　　　(마) ③

　　(나) 가능하면 밥은 혼자 먹지 말고 좋아하는
　　　　사람과 먹자.

　　(다) 여행은 다리가 떨릴 때 가지 말고 가슴이
　　　　떨릴 때 가자.

　　(라) 돈을 많이 벌려고만 하지 말고 잘 쓰는 방법을
　　　　생각해 보자.

　　(마) 다른 사람이 날 어떻게 볼까 걱정하지 말고
　　　　자신의 눈으로 세상을 보자.

22　바람이 불어　The Wind Blows

1　부는데 = 부 + 는데

　　흐르는데 = 흐르 + 는데

2　(나) 남산한옥마을에 가고 싶은데 길을 모른다.

　　(다) 지금 몇 시인데 아직까지 점심을 안 먹었니?

　　(라) 한국 음식을 좋아하는데 매운 건 못 먹는다.

(마) 요즘 한국 드라마를 보는데 자막이 없으면
　　안 된다.

(바) 한복을 처음 입어 봤는데 생각보다 가볍고
　　편했다.

23　비 뒤　After the Rain

1　반가운 비냐 = 반갑 + 은　비 +
　　　　　　　　　　　(이)냐

2　(나) 이 얼마나 예술적인 맛이냐.

　　(다) 이 얼마나 맑은 하늘이냐.

　　(라) 이 얼마나 감동적인 소설이냐.

　　(마) 이 얼마나 아름다운 소리냐.

　　(바) 이 얼마나 행복한 순간이냐.

24　사과　Apple

1　넷이서 = 넷 + 이서

2　(나) 셋이서 할 수 있는 보드게임을 알아?

　　(다) 넷이서 택시 한 대로 갈 수 있겠지?

　　(라) 다섯이서 이만 원씩 모으면 십만 원이 되겠다.

　　(마) 아홉이서 한데 다 묵으려면 펜션을 예약해야
　　　　겠다.

25　슬픈 족속　A Sorry People

1　흰 = 희 + ㄴ

　　검은 = 검 + 은

　　거친 = 거칠 + 은

　　슬픈 = 슬프 + ㄴ

　　가는 = 가늘 + 은

2　(나) 도둑　　　　　(다) 식사 대접
　　(라) 간호사　　　　(마) 한민족

26 서시 Prologue

1 사랑해야지 = 사랑하 + 여야 + 지

2 (나) 내 한글 이름을 예쁘게 지어야지.
(다) 예쁜 이름을 몇 개 선생님께 물어야지.
(라) 친구를 부를 때 한글 이름으로 불러야지.
(마) 내 이름을 짓고 나서 친구가 이름 짓는 걸
도와야지.

27 참새 Sparrows

1 쓰는걸 = 쓰 + 는 + 것 + 을

2 (나) 난 한식을 먹고 싶은걸.
(다) 난 불고기를 먹고 싶은걸.
(라) 난 고기를 더 먹고 싶은걸.
(마) 후회는 없어. 넓은 세상에 나와 세계를 알게
되었는걸.
(바) 당연하지. 그때 친구들이랑 참새를 잡으며
시간 가는 줄도 몰랐는걸.

28 남쪽 하늘 Southern Sky

1 그리운 = 그립 + 은
내리는 = 내리 + 는

2 (나) 윤동주는 대한민국을 대표하는, 한국
사람이 제일 좋아하는 시인 중 한 명이다.
(다) 〈남쪽 하늘〉은 1935년 10월 평양에서 쓰인,
서울에 대한 시인의 향수가 잘 드러난 작품이다.
(라) 이 시에서 제비의 두 날개는 가고 싶은 곳에
마음대로 가고 싶어 하는, 윤동주의 간절한
바람을 나타낸다.

29 밤 Night

1 어머니는 애기에게 = 어머니 + 는
애기 + 에게
먹이고 = 먹 + 이 + 고

2 (나) 엄마가 국을 끓여요.
(다) 엄마가 아이에게 밥을 먹여요.

(라) 엄마가 아이에게 옷을 입혀요.
(마) 엄마가 아이를 버스에 태워요.
(바) 엄마가 아이를 재워요.

30 눈 감고 간다
Go with your eyes closed

1 차이거든 = 차 + 이 + 거든

2 (나) ③, 레몬이 시거든 탄산수에 넣어서 마셔 봐.
(다) ⑤, 떡볶이가 맵거든 우유를 한 모금 드셔
보세요.
(라) ④, 약이 많이 쓰거든 초콜릿을 한 조각 드세요.
(마) ②, 삼계탕이 싱겁거든 소금을 좀 넣으세요.
(바) ①, 국이 그렇게 맛있거든 한 그릇 더 먹을래?

31 새벽이 올 때까지
Until the Dawn Arrives

1 울거들랑 = 울 + 거든 + 을랑

2 (나) 관광지에서 길을 잘 모르겠거들랑 길 찾기
앱을 이용해 봐.
(다) 밤에 잠 잘 숙소가 없거들랑 주변 찜질방을
검색해 보지 그래.
(라) 여행을 재미있게 하고 싶거들랑 미리
한국말을 좀 배워 가지고 가.
(마) 서울에서 대중교통으로 이동할 계획이거들랑
교통 카드를 사서 쓰는 게 좋아.
(바) 한국 사람과 함께 식사할 기회가 생기거들랑
윗사람이 수저를 들 때까지 기다리도록 해.

32 비행기 Airplane

1 찬 모양이야 = 차 + ㄴ 모양 +
이 + 야 *
찬가 봐 = 차 + ㄴ가 보 + 아 **

2 (나) 떡볶이가 매운 모양이야. /
떡볶이가 매운가 봐.
(다) 시험이 어려운 모양이야. /
시험이 어려운가 봐.
(라) 밖에 비가 많이 오는 모양이야. /
밖에 비가 많이 오나 봐.

(마) 강아지가 배가 고픈 모양이야. /
강아지가 배가 고픈가 봐.

33 창구멍 The Window's Opening

1 뚫어 논 = 뚫 + 어 놓 + 은

2 (나) 잡채를 해 놓았어요.
(다) 과일을 깎아 놓았어요.
(라) 케이크를 사 놓았어요.
(마) 미역국을 끓여 놓았어요.
(바) 창문에 풍선을 달아 놓았어요.

34 유언 Last Testament

1 갔다는 = 가 + 았 + 다(고 하) + 는
속삭인다는 = 속삭이 + ㄴ + 다(고 하)
+ 는

2 (나) ⑤, 내일은 비가 올 거라는 일기예보를 들었다.
(다) ①, 한국 시를 읽어 봤냐는 질문을 들었다.
(라) ③, 다시는 거짓말을 하지 않겠다는 약속을
들었다.
(마) ②, 영화를 보면서 한국어 공부를 해 보라는
조언을 들었다.

35 아우의 인상화
Portrait of a Younger Brother

1 사람이 되지 = 사람 + 이 되 + 지

2 (나) ①   (다) ⑤
(라) ③   (마) ④

36 사랑스런 추억 Beloved Memory

1 사랑처럼 = 사랑 + 처럼

2 (나) ①, 나는 체리처럼 빨간 립스틱을 발랐다.
(다) ⑤, 칠흑처럼 까만 밤하늘에 별 하나가 유난히
반짝거린다
(라) ④, 금덩어리처럼 노란 해가 석양빛 바다 위로
떨어진다.

(마) ②, 에메랄드처럼 파란 가을 하늘이 참
높기도 하다.

37 코스모스 Cosmos

1 어렸을 적처럼 = 어리 + 었 + 을
적 + 처럼

2 (나) ④, 아프던 강아지가 나았을 적처럼
다행스럽나니
(다) ⑤, 100m 달리기를 마쳤을 적처럼 가슴이
뛰나니
(라) ③, 모자에서 비둘기가 나왔을 적처럼
신기하나니
(마) ②, 첫사랑한테서 고백을 받았을 적처럼
설레나니
(바) ①, 길에서 우연히 옛 친구를 만났을 적처럼
반갑나니

38 자화상 Self-Portrait

1 미워져 = 밉 + 어지 + 어
가엾어집니다 = 가엾 + 어지 + ㅂ니다
그리워집니다 = 그립 + 어지 + ㅂ니다

2 (나) ③, 한국어를 배우고 나서 한국 친구가
많아졌다.
(다) ④, 밤을 새워 게임을 하고서 갑자기 내가
한심해졌다.
(라) ①, 한국어로 소설책을 읽는 속도가 빨라졌다.
(마) ⑤, 한국어로 시를 읽다니 내 자신이
자랑스러워졌다.

39 간판 없는 거리
A Road Without Signs

1 내렸을 = 내리 + 었 + 을

2 (나) 저는 가을에 단풍이 들었을 때 그리고 겨울에
눈이 올 때 거리 풍경이 참 아름다워 보입니다.
(다) 가게 주인은 해가 질 때부터 해가 뜰 때까지
(가게 일을 시작할 때부터 끝낼 때까지)
간판에 불을 켜 둡니다.

(라) 윤동주가 태어난 지 100년이 된 2017년 12월 30일 연변에 갔을 때 한글 간판을 봤어요. 중국 거리에 한글 간판이 많이 있는 것이 참 인상적이었어요.

(마) 모스크바에 갔을 때 본 지하철역이 기억에 남아요. 에스컬레이터로 땅 속 깊이 내려갔을 때 곳곳에 멋진 동상과 그림이 있었는데 마치 미술관에 온 것 같은 느낌이 들었거든요.

(라) ①, 윤동주는 문학을 공부하려고 서울로 유학을 떠났다.

(마) ④, 아픔을 겪은 사람들의 목소리를 전하려고 한강은 소설을 썼고 노벨 문학상을 받았다.

(바) ②, 누구나 쉽게 글로 의사소통을 하게 하려고 세종은 한글을 만들었다.

40 십자가 Cross

1 허락된다면 = 허락 + 되 + ㄴ + 다 + 면

2 (나) ④, 램프의 요정을 만난다면 첫 번째 소원으로 세계 평화를 빌 거야.

(다) ⑤, 한국어를 잘하게 된다면 제일 먼저 아이돌에게 팬레터를 쓸 거다.

(라) ⑥, 남한과 북한이 통일된다면 DMZ를 지나서 평양냉면을 먹으러 갈 거다.

(마) ①, 나이가 열 살쯤 어려진다면 악기 하나를 시작하고 싶다.

(바) ②, 휴가를 열흘쯤 낼 수 있다면 제주도 올레길을 돌아 보자.

41 간 Liver

1 뜯어먹어라 = 뜯 + 어 + 먹 + 어 + 라

2 (나) 달아, 구름 밖으로 나와라.

(다) 비야, 이제 그만 멈춰라.

(라) 나무야, 누워서 자라.

(마) 나비야, 이리 날아 오너라.

42 햇빛 · 바람 Sunlight·Wind

1 내다보려 = 내다보 + 려 (+ 고)

2 (나) ⑥, 토끼는 용왕을 속이려고 바위 위에 간을 꺼내 두고 왔다고 거짓말을 했다.

(다) ⑤, 혼자 한국어를 공부해 보려고 이 책을 사서 연습 중이다.

43 츠르게네프의 언덕 Turgenev's Hill

1 이야기나 = 이야기 + 나

2 (나) 빨래나 할까?

(다) 컵라면이나 할까?

(라) 다시 잠이나 잘까?

(마) 친구나 만나러 나갈까?

(바) 태블릿으로 영화나 볼까?

44 소년 The Boy

1 쓸어 보면 = 쓸 + 어 보 + 면

들여다본다 = 들이 + 어다 + 보 + ㄴ다

감아 본다 = 감 + 아 보 + ㄴ다

2 (나) 사귀어 보면

(다) 지내 보자면서

(라) 노력해 봤지만

(마) 감아 봐도

45 위로 Comfort

1 파득거려도 = 파득거리 + 어도

감기우기만 한다 = 감 + 기 + 우 + 기 + 만 하 + ㄴ다

2 (나) 약을 먹어도 나빠지기만 했다.

(다) 쉬어도 피곤하기만 했다.

(라) 방 온도를 높여도 춥기만 했다.

(마) 열심히 공부하라고 해도 놀기만 했다.

(바) 손부터 씻으라고 해도 그냥 먹기만 했다.

46 병원 Hospital

1 기울도록 = 기울 + 도록

2 (나) ⑥, 이 나이가 되도록 외국어 하나 제대로
　　　 못 배운 것이 후회가 된다.
　　 (다) ②, 한 시간이 지나도록 배달 음식이 안 온다.
　　 (라) ⑤, 수도관이 얼지 않도록 겨울에는 야외
　　　 공원의 수도 시설을 잠가 둔다.
　　 (마) ①, 해가 하늘 중천에 뜨도록 늦잠을 잤다.
　　 (바) ④, 윤동주의 시를 잘 이해하도록 이 책에는
　　　 영어 번역본을 덧붙였다.

47 무서운 시간 A Frightening Time

1 떨어질 텐데 = 떨어지 + 을 터 +
　　　　　　　　　　　　 이 + ㄴ데

2 (나) ⑥, 미세 먼지가 건강에 안 좋을 텐데 외출할
　　　 때는 항상 마스크를 챙기세요.
　　 (다) ③, 출근 시간이라서 차가 밀릴 텐데 30분
　　　 일찍 출발해야겠다.
　　 (라) ②, 제가 떠나면 많이 섭섭하실 텐데 자주
　　　 연락드리겠습니다.
　　 (마) ⑤, 오래 앉아 있으면 허리가 아플 텐데 가끔
　　　 스트레칭이라도 해라.
　　 (바) ④, 이사 와서 아는 사람도 많이 없을 텐데
　　　 오다가다 종종 들르세요.

48 쉽게 씌어진 시
A Poem Easily Written

1 천명인 줄 알면서도

　　 = 천명 + 이 + ㄴ 줄 알 +
　　　 면서 + 도

2 (나) ④, 내 체력으로 무리인 줄 알면서도 산
　　　 정상까지 오를 계획을 세웠다.
　　 (다) ①, 친구의 말이 농담인 줄 알면서도
　　　 생각할수록 기분이 나쁘다.
　　 (라) ②, 거짓말을 하면 안 되는 줄 알면서도
　　　 할머니를 속일 수밖에 없었다.

　　 (마) ⑥, 이맘때 엄마 생일이 있는 줄 알면서도
　　　 회사 일이 바빠서 잊고 말았다.
　　 (바) ③, 떠나보내고 나서 후회할 줄 알면서도
　　　 아이가 원하는 유학을 허락했다.

49 참회록 Confession

1 밤이면 밤마다 = 밤 + 이 + 면
　　　　　　　　　　　　 밤 + 마다

2 (나) ①, 방이면 방마다 투숙객이 가득해
　　　 만원이었다.
　　 (다) ③, 봄이면 봄마다 베란다의 군자란이
　　　 꽃을 피운다.
　　 (라) ⑤, 밤이면 밤마다 달님을 보며 고향집
　　　 안부를 묻는다.
　　 (마) ②, 가방이면 가방마다 아이의 이름표가
　　　 붙어 있었다.

50 별 헤는 밤
A Night Counting Stars

1 쉬이 = 쉽 + 이

　　 아슬히 = 아슬 + 히

　　 피어나듯이 = 피 + 어나 + 듯 + 이

2 (나) ④, 지하철은 분주히 출근하는 사람들로
　　　 만원이었다.
　　 (다) ②, 줄리엣은 반듯이 누워서 천장을 올려다
　　　 보았다.
　　 (라) ③, 네가 마신 물컵은 깨끗이 닦아서 선반
　　　 위에 올려 두어라.
　　 (마) ①, 경주는 불교문화가 찬란히 꽃피어 있는
　　　 관광지이다.
　　 (바) ⑤, 이모는 따뜻이 내 손을 잡으며 안부를
　　　 물으셨다.

01 봄 1 Spring 1

N에/에서

장소 명사 뒤에 붙는 조사이다. '에'는 어떤 명사의 상태가 유지되는 장소 명사 뒤에 붙여서 '있다, 없다' 등 형용사(DV)와 함께 쓰고 '에서'는 어떤 행동이 일어나는 장소 명사 뒤에 붙여서 동사(AV)와 함께 쓴다.

Grammar Tip

'정확한' 또는 '한창인'의 뜻을 더하는 접두사이다.

02 못 자는 밤 Sleepless Nights

-도 하다

부사나 형용사 어간에 붙여 써서 감탄이나 놀라움을 나타낸다. 형용사 어간 뒤에 붙일 때는 명사형 어미 '기'를 붙여서 '-기도 하다'로 쓰거나 부사화 접미사 '-이, -게' 다음에 '도'를 붙여서 사용한다. '둘이서 저녁을 많이도 먹었구나, 아이가 참 슬프게도 운다.'처럼 '도' 뒤에는 '하다' 대신에 다른 여러 가지 동사를 쓸 수도 있다.

03 무얼 먹고 사나
What Do They Live Off Of?

Background Knowledge

이 시가 실린 『가톨릭소년』은 천주교 만주연길교구에서 소년 · 소녀들을 대상으로 1934년부터 1940년까지 발간된 월간 잡지이다. 주로 교회사 · 서양사 · 과학기술 · 청소년 문제 등 소년 · 소녀를 위한 교양물과 지혜주머니 · 기담(奇談) · 오락실 · 동화 · 동요 · 동시 · 소설 등의 내용을 실었다.

Nㄹ

모음으로 끝난 명사 뒤에는 목적격 조사 '을/를' 대신에 'ㄹ'만 붙여도 목적어가 된다. 하지만 보고서 같은 공적인 글에는 이와 같이 줄여 쓰지 않는다.

04 나무 Tree

Background Knowledge

시 〈나무〉의 재미는 과학적인 인과 관계를 거꾸로 뒤집은 데 있다. 바람이 불어서 나무가 흔들리는 것인데 나무가 춤을 추기 때문에 바람이 분다고 생각한 스무 살 시인의 생각이 재미있다. 독립을 염원하던 시인은 한 사람 한 사람이 잠잠히 있지 말고 행동에 나서야 해방의 큰 바람을 불러일으킬 수 있다고 믿었다.

V1(으)면 V2

불확실한 상황을 가정하거나 특정한 상황일 때만 어떤 일이 일어난다고 말하고 싶을 때 그러한 상황에 대해 '-(으)면'을 써서 한정한다.

05 산울림 Echo

Background Knowledge

윤동주에게는 육필 자선 시집 『하늘과 바람과 별과 시』 이외에도 4개의 습작 노트가 더 있다. 윤동주는 두 번째 묶음집에 '창(窓)'이라는 제목을 붙이고 '햇빛 · 바람, 해바라기 얼굴, 애기의 새벽, 귀뚜라미와 나와, 산울림' 등 5편의 동시를 포함시켰다. 1938년 4월 그가 연변에서 연희전문학교가 있는 서울로 유학을 떠나면서 동시 창작은 중단된다. 서울에서 연변과 다른 문학적 환경에 놓이게 되고 조선일보에 '아우의 인상화(1939. 10.17.)'가 실리면서 자신의 시적 가능성을 확인하게 된 것이 동시 창작을 중단한 원인으로 추정된다.

못 AV

어떤 동작을 할 수 없다거나 상태가 이루어지지 않았음을 나타내는 부사이다. 말할 때는 '못 AV'와 같이 '못'을 앞에 써서 짧게 말하고, 글을 쓸 때는 주로 'AV지 못하다'와 같이 동사 뒤에 붙여 긴 부정문 형태로 쓴다.

Grammar Tip

'-는다, -ㄴ다, -냐, -어라, -자'와 같은 종결 어미로서, ('이다'의 어간, 형용사 어간 또는 어미 '-으시-', '-었-', '-겠-' 뒤에 붙어) 어떤 사건이나 사실, 상태를 서술하는 데 쓰인다.

06　식권　Meal Ticket

Background Knowledge

한국어에서 '-모(母)'로 끝나는 단어는 돈을 벌기 위해 남의 집에 들어가서 어떤 일을 주로 맡아 하는 여자라는 뜻을 나타낸다. 예를 들어, 옷을 바느질하는 '침모(針母)', 반찬을 만드는 '찬모(餐母)', 주인집 아이에게 친어머니 대신 젖을 먹이는 '유모(乳母)' 등은 조선 시대까지 가난한 여자들이 주로 하던 직업이었다. 이 시에 나오는 '식모(食母)'는 남의 집에 고용되어 부엌일을 하는 여자라는 의미의 단어로, 1970년대까지도 남아 있었던 직업이다. 1980년대까지 한국의 웬만한 주택과 아파트에는 부엌방이 따로 있어서 식모를 들이는 경우 주거 공간으로 제공하곤 하였다.

N(으)로

어떤 물건의 재료를 나타내는 격 조사이다. 받침 없는 명사 뒤에서는 '로'를 쓴다. 'ㄹ' 받침으로 끝나는 명사 뒤에서도 '으' 없이 '로'만 쓴다.

07　병아리　Chicks

Background Knowledge

윤동주가 시작 활동을 본격화한 것은 1936년이며 이 시기에 그가 주력한 장르는 동시이다. 이 동시 〈병아리〉와 〈빗자루〉가 당시 연길에서 간행되던 『가톨릭 소년』이라는 잡지에 1936년 11월과 12월에 잇달아 발표된 것을 보면, 당시 연변의 문학 매체가 소년 잡지였기 때문에 동시 창작을 주력으로 했을 가능성이 있다.

V어/아/여.

자신의 말을 듣는 사람이 자신과 나이가 같거나 어린 경우 또는 나이가 많아도 아주 가까운 사이일 때에 사용하는 반말 종결어미이다. 말할 때 주로 사용하는 이 반말 형태는 서술, 질문, 요청, 청유의 형태가 모두 똑같다.

08　가슴 3　Heart 3

ㄹ 동사

동사 어간이 /ㄹ/ 로 끝나는 동사들을 가리킨다. 이러한 ㄹ 불규칙 동사는 /ㅅ, ㄴ, ㅂ/ 앞에서 /ㄹ/이 없어진다.

Rhetoric Tip

ㄹ 불규칙 동사: 어간의 끝소리인 'ㄹ'이 'ㄴ', 'ㅂ', 'ㅅ'으로 시작하는 어미나 어미 '-오' 앞에서 없어진다. '길다'가 '기니', '깁니다', '기오'로 바뀌는 것이 그러한 예이다.

불규칙 동사가 어떻게 활용되는지 연습해 보자.

09　할아버지　Grandfather

V다고 하오.

간접 화법에서 나이 많은 어른이 역시 나이가 적지 않은 상대방을 존중하면서 반말을 할 때 '하오체'를 쓴다. '-오, -소, -구려'체는 옛날에 많이 쓰던 표현이기 때문에 옛날 배경의 드라마에서 많이 들을 수 있다. 전해 들은 말의 내용이 설명, 질문, 요청, 청유 중에서 어느 것이냐에 따라서 '-다고, -냐고, -으라고, -자고' 등으로 달라질 수 있으며, '합니다, 해요'와 같은 의미의 '하오'와 연결해서 말한다.

10　호주머니　Pockets

N만 V(으)면

'-(으)면' 앞에 있는 'N만'은 어떤 상태를 만들기 위해서 최소로 필요한 조건임을 표시한다. '-(으)면'과 함께 써서 그 조건이 있을 때는 언제나 같은 상황이 반복될 수 있음을 나타낸다.

반어법: 실제로 전달하고 싶은 의미와 반대로 말을 해서 그 의미를 강조하는 수사법입니다. 아이가 잘못했을 때 엄마가 화를 내면서 "참 잘했다!"라고 말하거나 예쁜 아이를 보고 "참 얄밉게 생겼다."라고 말하는 것이 그러한 예입니다. 이러한 맥락에서 윤동주가 이 시에서 겨울에 주먹 두 개로만 채워진 호주머니를 강조한 이유를 아래 질문들을 통해 생각해 봅시다.

- 윤동주가 살았던 1917-1945년 한국의 겨울 날씨는 어땠을까요?

- 그 때 사람들은 추운 겨울에 무엇이 필요했을까요?

- 빈 호주머니에 주먹 두 개만 꽉 차 있는 사람의 기분은 어떨까요?

- 주머니 안에 아무 것도 없는 사람을 보는 시인의 마음은 어땠을까요?

11 개 1 Dog 1

Background Knowledge

이 시가 재미있는 이유는 '꽃을 그리다'가 2개의 의미로 해석되기 때문이다. '그리다'는 '사랑하는 마음으로 간절히 생각하다, 연필 등으로 사물의 모양을 선이나 색으로 나타내다'의 뜻을 가진 단어이다. 시인은 눈 위에서 강아지가 팔짝팔짝 뛰면서 꽃처럼 생긴 발자국을 남기는 것을 보면서 꽃 그림을 그린다고 묘사하는 한편 강아지가 꽃을 그리워하기 때문에 뛰는 것처럼 해석될 수도 있게 말장난을 담았다.

부사구의 위치

부사구란 둘 이상의 단어가 모여서 부사처럼 동사의 의미를 상세히 설명하는 데 쓰이는 구절이다. '철수는 아주 열심히 산다.'에서 '아주 열심히'와 '산다'의 관계처럼 보통 부사구는 서술어(형용사, 동사 등) 바로 앞에, 즉 서술어와 가까운 자리에 쓰인다. 그런데 이 시에서처럼 '눈 위에서'라는 부사구를 문장의 제일 앞에 쓰면 '눈 위에서'가 '뛴다'라는 동사 하나가 아니라 문장 전체를 꾸미는 역할을 하게 된다. 이 시에서는 장소를 나타내는 부사구의 음절이 총 4개가 되면서 글자 수가 '4-2-5-2'로 맞춰져 자연스럽게 리듬이 만들어졌다.

12 오줌싸개 지도 Map of the Bedwetter

N인가, AV는가, DV은가/ㄴ가?

현재 사실에 대한 의문이나 놀람을 나타내는 종결 어미이다. 특히 '-는가'는 '있다', '없다', '계시다'의 어간이나 동사의 어간 그리고 어미 '-으시-', '-었-', '-겠-' 뒤에 붙어 현재 상황이나 사실에 대한 질문을 만든다. 질문을 할 때 많이 쓰는 의문사, 즉 '누가, 언제, 어디, 무엇' 등과 자주 함께 쓰인다. 반대되는 정보를 연달아 써서 대조의 의미를 강조할 수 있다.

13 이불 Blanket

N1(이)랑 N2(이)랑 DV어하다

명사들(N1, N2)이 주변의 대상에 대하여 형용사가 뜻하는 느낌을 나타낸다는 의미이다. 예를 들어 이 시에서는 '지붕'과 '길'과 '밭'이 날씨를 추워하는 것 같다고 아이가 생각하는 것이다. 이처럼 형용사 어근에 '-어하다'를 붙이면 동사가 된다. 조사 '이랑'과 '하고'는 말할 때 사용하고, 같은 뜻을 가진 '와/과'는 글을 쓸 때 주로 사용한다. 이러한 조사들은 주로 명사 두 개를 연결할 때 쓰이지만 문장에 서술된 행동을 할 대상이나 비교 기준을 나타내기도 한다.

Rhetoric Tip

활유법: 활유법은 무생물을 생물인 것처럼, 감정이 없는 것을 감정이 있는 사람처럼 표현하는 수사법이다. '나를 둘러싼 산', '울음 우는 바다' 등이 그러한 예이다. 이 시에서 윤동주는 어린이의 마음으로 지붕과 길과 밭 위에 내린 눈을 보고서 세상이 추워한다고 누군가 솜이불처럼 하얀 눈을 덮어 주었다고 묘사하였다.

14 그 여자 That Woman

V어/아 (가지고)

'-어/아 가지고'는 앞말이 뜻하는 행동이나 상태가 끝난 결과가 그대로 유지되거나, 앞말의 행동이나 상태 때문에 뒷말의 행동이나 상태가 가능하게 되었음을 나타낸다. 문어체보다는 구어체에 많이 사용되며 '가지고'는 '갖고'로 줄여 쓰거나 아예 안 쓰는 경우도 많다.

15 해바라기 얼굴 Sunflower-like Face

AV자(마자)

앞 동작이 이루어졌을 때 잇따라 다음 사건이나 동작이 일어남을 나타내는 연결 어미이다. '-자'만 남기고 '마자'를 생략해서 쓸 수도 있다. 하지만 곧바로 이어서 다음 상황이 일어난다는 즉시적 시간의 의미는 약해진다. '-자(마자)'와 비슷한 의미를 가진 '-는 대로'는 미래의 계획을 말할 때만 쓴다는 점에서 다르다.

16 가슴 2 Heart 2

V(으)ㅁ

동사를 명사로 만들어 주는 어미이다. '잠을 자다/꿈을 꾸다/그림을 그리다'처럼 동사의 어간에 '음/ㅁ'을 붙여서 명사로 만든다. '-(으)ㅁ' 말고도 동사를 명사로 만들어 주는 표현은 '-기, '-는/은/을 것' 이 있다. 이와 같이 명사형으로 끝나는 문장은 한 일이나 할 일을 적는 메모 또는 여러 사람에게 보이기 위한 게시판 글에서 자주 볼 수 있다. 보통 현재나 과거의 일에는 '-음'을, 미래의 계획이나 결심에는 '-기'를 그리고 'N1(주어) = N2(용언)이다' 구문에서 주어가 긴 경우에 '-는/은/을 것' 형태를 쓴다.

17 반딧불 Fireflies

Background Knowledge

이 시를 쓴 1937년에 윤동주는 광명중학교 농구 선수로 활약했다. 이 해 그는 아버지와 진로 문제로 갈등이 있었다. 아버지는 의대나 법대 진학을 강력하게 원했지만 그는 문과 진학을 고집하였다. 아버지와 매일이 문제를 두고 충돌해서 집에서 밥그릇, 물그릇이 날아다닐 정도였다고 한다. 손자를 아끼던 할아버지가 그의 편을 들어 주어서 윤동주는 1938년 연희전문학교(현재 연세대학교) 문과에 진학할 수 있게 되었다. 1938년 10월에 투고하여 1939년 1월에 〈조선일보〉에 실린 "달을 쏘다"라는 그의 수필을 보면, 가을 달밤에 연세대학교 연못에 비친 달을 보고 나뭇가지로 새총을 만들어 달을 쏘는 장면이 나온다. 이 시에서 가을 반딧불을 보고 달 조각이라 여길 만큼 스무 살 즈음의 윤동주는 달과 달빛, 달그림자에 대한 관심이 많았던 것으로 보인다.

AV(으)러 N(으)로 가자

'-(으)러'는 어떤 장소로 가거나 오는 동작의 목적을 나타내는 연결 어미이고 '-자'는 어떤 행동을 함께하자고 청유하는 뜻을 나타내는 반말 종결 어미이다. 청유하는 행동이 일어날 장소를 특별히 강조할 때 'N에'를 쓸 수 있는데, 'N에'는 좁게 바로 그 장소만을 가리키는 반면, 'N으로'를 쓰면 그 장소가 있는 쪽을 광범위하게 가리키는 의미이다.

18 산협의 오후 Mountain Valley Afternoon

A/V는구나., DV구나.

나이가 어린 청자에게나 혹은 스스로에게, 감탄하는 내용을 전달할 때 쓴다. 주로 나보다 어린 사람에게 사용하는 반말의 종류에는 격식체 반말과 비격식체 반말이 있다. 'AV는다./DV다./N이다' 등의 격식체 반말은 공식적인 서술문에 주로 쓰이고, 그 이외의 'V니?/AV어라/AV자/AV는구나/DV구나' 같은 격식체 질문, 요청, 청유, 감탄의 의미를 나타내는 반말은 나이 차이가 많이 나는 윗사람이 아랫사람에게, 혹은 아주 친한 관계에서만 사용한다. 'V어/아/여.' 형태의 비격식체 반말은 보통 나이가 같은 동갑 사이에 많이 사용한다.

19 고향집 — 만주에서 부른 My Home — Called for from Manchuria

Background Knowledge

1936년에 쓰인 이 시에서 윤동주는 만주에서 두만강 건너 한반도 남쪽의 고향을 그리워하고 있다. 즉, 그의 국적은 한반도에 있는 나라인 것이다.

AV고, AV어/아서

의미상 앞뒤 행동의 순서를 바꿀 수 없는 경우 '-어서'를 써서 연결한다. 하지만 '어깨에 가방을 메다, 운동화 끈을 매다, 슬리퍼를 끌다'처럼 몸에 직접 닿는 동사, 즉 '신체 부착 동사'의 행동 순서를 나타낼 때에는 동사 어간에 '-고'를 붙여서 뒤의 다른 행동과 연결해야 한다. 한편, '-고'는 보통 '먼저 숙제하고 그 후에 놀자, 먼저 놀고 나서 그 다음에 숙제할 것이다.'처럼 순서를 바꾸어도 되는 행동들을 연결할 때 쓴다.

 새로운 길 A New Path

Background Knowledge

윤동주는 이 시가 창작되기 3달 전인 1938년 2월에 광명중학교 5학년을 졸업하고 4월에 연희전문학교 문과에 입학해서 3년간 기숙사 생활을 했다. 최현배, 이양하 교수에게서 배웠고 1938년 여름 방학 때는 용정 북부교회에서 여름성경학교 교사를 했다.

현재 서울에 있는 연세대학교 신촌캠퍼스에는 '청송대'라는 소나무 숲이 있다. 이 숲 근처에는 1980년까지 문과대학으로 쓰이던 본관이 있다. 아마도 윤동주는 기숙사(현 윤동주 기념관)를 나와서 문과대학(현 본관)에서 공부하고 청송대의 자연 환경을 보며 자기 인생의 '새로운 길'에 대한 결심을 세웠을 것이다.

N(으)로

주어가 목표로 삼아 움직이는 방향을 나타내는 격 조사이다. 'ㄹ' 받침으로 끝나거나 모음으로 끝나는 명사 뒤에는 '로'를 쓴다. '(으)로'는 도구나 재료를 나타내는 데 쓰이기도 한다.

21 귀뚜라미와 나와
The Cricket and I

AV지 말고 AV자.

선행절의 행동(동사)을 하지 못하게 하고 후행절의 다른 행동(동사)을 하도록 권하는 표현이다. 어떤 부정적인 행동 대신 새로운 긍정적인 행동을 하라고 권유할 때는 'AV1지 말고 AV2어라.'를 쓰고, 말하는 사람과 함께 하기를 바라는 내용일 때는 'AV1지 말고 AV2자.'를 쓴다. 상대방에게 부드럽게 권유하거나 스스로에게 하는 말일 경우에는 'AV어야지, AV어야겠다'처럼 결심을 나타내는 표현을 덧붙인다.

22 바람이 불어 The Wind Blows

AV는데/DV은데/N인데

후행절 상황의 어떠한 배경을 밝힐 때나 후행절 상황과 대조되는 내용을 설명하기 위하여 후행절과 관계 있는 상황을 선행절에 미리 제시할 때에 쓰는 연결 어미이다.

23 비 뒤 After the Rain

Background Knowledge

청년 윤동주는 정지용(1902-1950) 시인의 시에서 여러 모로 영향을 받았다. 두 시 모두 농사를 짓는 할아버지를 보는 아이의 시선으로 쓰였다는 공통점이 있다. 정지용의 〈할아버지〉라는 시에도 이 시와 같이, '할아버지, 담배, 비' 같은 소재가 등장한다. 다만 차이점은 정지용의 시에 나오는 아이는 할아버지가 그날의 날씨를 어떻게 알고 날씨에 딱 맞게 옷을 입고 나서시는지 놀라워하기만 하고 있다는 것이다. 하지만 윤동주의 시 〈할아버지〉에 나오는 아이는 오랫만에 내리는 비를 할아버지와 함께 반가워하며 아름답게 여기고 곡식의 강인한 생명력을 선명한 청각적 이미지로 전달하고 있다.

(N1은/는) 얼마나 DV(으)ㄴ N2(이)냐

동작이나 상태의 정도가 아주 큼을 나타내는 부사 '얼마나'와 의문형 종결어미 '-냐'를 써서 '주어의 상태나 정도를 강조하는 표현이다. N2는 N1이 속한 범주를 가리키는 단어이고, 생략된 주어 N1에 대한 놀라움을 부각하기 위하여 'DV은/ㄴ N2'로 순서를 바꾸었다. 생략된 N1의 자리에 '이'를 쓰기도 한다. 예를 들어, '한국어가 아주 어렵다.'라고 강조하고 싶다면 '(한국어는) 이 얼마나 어려운 언어인가.'라고 바꾸어 표현한다. '-냐' 대신에 의문형 종결 어미 '-니'를 쓰면 동의를 구하는 느낌이 강해지고 '-는가'를 쓰면 놀라움의 의미가 강해진다.

24 사과 Apple

N이서

'혼자, 둘, 셋, 넷'처럼 수를 나타내는 명사에 붙여서 그 말이 주어임을 나타내는 격 조사이다. 명사가 사람의 수를 나타낼 때에만 사용하며 문어에는 쓰지 않고 주로 구어적 상황에만 쓴다.

25 슬픈 족속 A Sorry People

Background Knowledge

"시인이(유정물 + 주격 조사) 시를(무정물 + 목적격 조사) 쓴다.(동사)"처럼 한국어 문장에서는 감정을 느낄 수 있는 인격 주체가 주어 자리에 오는 것이 자연스럽다. '만두가 아이에게 먹힌다.'보다 '아이가 만두를 먹는다.'가 좋은 문장인 이유는 감정을 느낄 수 있는 '아이'가 '만두'보다 주어 자리에 더 잘 어울리기 때문이다. 하지만 시에서 이러한 문법 규칙을 깨트리면 수사적으로 신선한 느낌을 줄 수 있다.

-는/은/ㄴ/을/ㄹ N

동사나 형용사에 붙여서 뒤의 명사를 꾸미는 관형형 어미이다. 시제와 어간의 받침 유무에 따라서 다르게 쓴다. 동사의 과거 관형형에는 '-은/ㄴ', 현재 관형형에는 '-는', 미래 관형형에는 '-을/ㄹ'을 붙이고 형용사의 관형형에는 '-은/ㄴ'을 붙인다. 동사나 형용사 어간이 모음으로 끝난 경우에는 '으' 없이 'ㄴ'이나 'ㄹ'만 쓴다.

26 서시 Prologue

Background Knowledge

이 시는 제목이 '서시'로 알려져 있는데, 사실은 윤동주가 스스로 골라서 시집으로 묶은 19편 시 가운데 제일 앞에 놓인 작품이어서 '서시'로 불리게 된 것이다.

AV어/아야지

청자가 해야 할 의무에 대해 동의를 구하는 뜻을 나타내는 종결 어미이다. 혼잣말로 화자의 의지를 나타내기도 한다. '나도 가지. 늦었는데 이제 그만 일어나지.'처럼 'V지.'는 어미 '-으시-', '-었-', '-겠-' 뒤에 붙여, 어떤 사실을 긍정적으로 서술하거나 묻거나 명령하거나 제안하는 뜻을 나타내는 종결 어미이다.

27 참새 Sparrows

Background Knowledge

북간도 용정의 윤동주 생가 마당 한 편에는 시 '참새'가 다른 시들과 함께 액자에 걸려 있다. 윤동주는 어린 시절 북간도 용정에서 송몽규와 함께 자랐다. 송몽규는 윤동주의 고종 사촌으로 윤동주보다 먼저 문단에 등단했고 같이 일본 유학도 떠났으며 일본에 유학을 온 학생들을 모아 독립 활동을 하면서 윤동주의 일생에 많은 영향을 끼쳤다. 흑백 영화 〈동주〉(2016)를 보면 송몽규의 독립 투지와 윤동주의 시적 감성을 잘 느낄 수 있다.

V는걸

현재의 사실이 이미 알고 있는 정보나 기대와 다름을 나타내는 종결 어미이다. 가벼운 반박이나 지나간 일에 대한 후회, 감탄의 뜻을 나타낸다. 과거를 나타낼 때는 '-었는걸.', 형용사에는 '- DV(으)ㄴ 걸.', 명사에는 'N인걸.'을 쓴다.

28 남쪽 하늘 Southern Sky

(N1이/가) V1는,

문장에서 쉼표는 관형절의 원격 수식을 나타내는 기호이다. 보통 형용사에는 어간 받침의 유무와 추측성 여부에 따라 '-은/ㄴ/을' 붙이고, 동사에는 과거, 현재, 미래 시제에 따라 '-은/는/을'을 붙인 뒤에 바로 뒤의 명사를 꾸민다. 만약 꾸미는 내용을 가진 관형절과 꾸밈을 받는 명사가 앞뒤에 바로 이어져 있지 않다면 관형절 뒤에 '쉼표(,)'를 써서 멀리 있는 명사를 수식하는 관계임을 밝혀야 한다.

29 밤 Night

사동 표현

사동형 접사 '-이/히/리/기/우/구/추-'가 붙은 사동사는, N1이 N2에게 N3이 포함된 어떤 동작이나 행동을 하게 시키는 의미를 갖는다.

30 눈 감고 간다 Go with your eyes closed

V거든

'어떤 일이 사실이면', '어떤 일이 사실로 실현되면'이라는 뜻을 나타내는 연결 어미이다.

31 새벽이 올 때까지
Until the Dawn Arrives

Background Knowledge

이 시가 쓰인 1941년 5월부터 윤동주는 학교 기숙사를 나와서 소설가 김송 집에서 하숙을 했다. 이 해에 윤동주는 릴케, 발레리, 지드 등 외국 문학 작품을 탐독하였고 프랑스어 자습(공부)을 시작하였다.

V거들랑

'어떤 일이 사실이면', '어떤 일이 사실로 드러나면'이라는 뜻을 나타내는 연결 어미로서 주로 청유형 어미와 함께 쓰인다. 어미 '-거든'과 조사 '을랑'이 결합한 표현이다. '을랑'은 반말 사용이 가능한 가까운 사이에서 쓰이며 특별한 상황을 한정하는 뜻을 갖는다. '-거들랑'이 문장의 끝에서 종결 어미로 쓰이면 청자는 모르고 있는 내용을 가르쳐 준다는 부연 설명의 기능을 한다. '-걸랑'으로 줄여 쓸 수 있다.

32 비행기 Airplane

AV는 모양이다

추측을 나타내는 종결 어미이다. 동사의 과거나 형용사와 결합할 때에는 'A/V은/ㄴ 모양이다'라고 쓴다. 'AV나/DV은가/N인가 보다/싶다'도 추측의 뜻을 나타내지만 'AV는 모양이다'는 시청각 정보를 바탕으로 좀 더 구체적으로 추측할 때 사용한다.

Rhetoric Tip

*-야: ('이다, 아니다' 어간 뒤에 쓰여서) 사실을 서술하거나 물을 때 쓰는 종결 어미이다.

**-어/아/여: 어떤 사실을 서술하거나 물음·명령·청유의 뜻을 나타내는 종결 어미이다.

33 창구멍 The Window's Opening

Background Knowledge

이 시 〈창구멍〉은 1938년 〈햇빛·바람〉으로 개작되었다. 두 시를 비교해 보고 무엇이 같고 다른지 그 느낌을 비교해 보자.

AV어/아 놓다

동사의 행동을 끝내고 행동이 끝난 결과를 그대로 유지함을 나타내는 보조 동사이다.

34 유언 Last Testament

V다는 N

명사(N)를 꾸미는 '-다는'은 '-다고 하는'이 줄어든 말로서, 다른 사람한테서 들은 내용을 옮겨 전할 때 사용하는 간접 인용 표현이다. 들은 말이 질문이면 '-냐는', 부탁이면 '-으라는', 청하는 말이면 '-자는'을 쓴다. 부탁하는 사람이 간청하기 위하여 사용한 '좀'과 같은 부사어는 빼고 들은 내용을 요약해서 전달하는 것이 좋다.

35 아우의 인상화
Portrait of a Younger Brother

Background Knowledge

인상화란 인상주의 화풍으로 그려진 그림을 가리킨다. 인상주의는 19세기 후반 프랑스에서 일어난 근대 미술의 한 경향으로, 있는 그대로의 사물을 사실적으로 재현하기보다 사물에서 작가가 받은 순간적인 인상을 주관적으로 대담하게 표현하는 것을 목적으로 하였다. 그 결과 사물의 고유색을 부정하고 태양 광선에 의하여 시시각각으로 변해 보이는 대상의 순간적인 색채를 포착하는 화풍을 유행시켰다. 드가, 르누아르, 마네, 모네 등이 대표적 작가이다.

V지

청자가 이미 알고 있는 사실에 대해 화자가 긍정적으로 서술할 때 사용하는 종결 어미이다. 그리고 화자의 동의를 구하는 부드러운 태도를 보이면서 부탁, 제안을 할 때에도 사용한다. 화자와 청자 간에 서로 알고 있는 주제에 대하여 화자가 확실히 알지 못하는 정보를 부드러운 태도로 청자에게 다시 확인하는 의문문에도 사용한다.

36 사랑스런 추억 *Beloved Memory*

Background Knowledge

이 시는 릿교대학 용지에 작성되었다. 윤동주는 1942년 4월에 동경 릿교대학 문학부 영문과에 입학해서 '흰 그림자, 흐르는 거리, 사랑스런 추억, 쉽게 쓰여진 시, 봄' 등 시 5편을 릿교대 용지에 써서 서울에 있는 친구 강처중에게 보냈다. 1942년 10월에 윤동주는 도시샤 대학 영문과로 옮겨 공부를 이어 갔다. 1943년 여름 방학 귀향을 앞둔 7월14일에 '치안 유지법 위반 혐의'로 교토 시모가모 경찰서에 체포되어 기소된 그는 징역 2년형을 받고 후쿠오카 형무소에 투옥됐지만 1945년 2월16일 27세의 젊은 나이로 옥사했다.

N처럼

모양이 서로 비슷하거나 같음을 나타내는 격 조사이다. N1과 N2의 속성 가운데 비슷한 것을 강조할 때 쓴다.

37 코스모스 *Cosmos*

V1었을 적처럼 V2나니

'적'은 일부 명사나 어미 '-(으)ㄴ, -을' 뒤에 쓰여서 그 동작이 진행되거나 그 상태가 나타나 있는 시기 또는 지나간 어떤 시기라는 의미의 의존 명사이다. 그리고 '-나니'는 '-기 때문에'와 비슷하게 앞말이 뒷말의 원인이나 근거, 전제가 됨을 설명하는 옛 표현이다.

38 자화상 *Self-Portrait*

DV어/아지다

형용사 어간이 뜻하는 상태로 됨을 나타내는 보조 동사이다.

39 간판 없는 거리 *A Road Without Signs*

Background Knowledge

1941년 12월 27일 윤동주는 연희전문학교를 졸업했다. 당시 기차를 타고 다니는 여행객과 헌 와사등을 밝히고 가게에서 손님을 기다리는 사람들의 경제적 여건은 많이 달랐다. 윤동주가 유학한 도시에는 어디에나 있는, "빨갛게 파랗게 불붙는 문자(네온사인)"가 그의 고향에는 없었다. 하지만 그런 간판이 없어도 익숙한 고향 거리에서는 집을 못 찾을까 봐 걱정하지 않아도 된다. 이 시에는 그런 고향의 사람들에 대한 윤동주의 애정이 잘 드러나 있다. 마지막 연의 끝맺지 않은 문장에는 봄, 여름, 가을, 겨울 사계절 내내 플랫폼으로 들어오는 기차와 기차에서 내리는 손님의 영원한 순환 구조가 나타난다.

V(었/았)을 때

'때'는 어떤 일이나 사건이 일어나는 시간을 나타내는 명사이다. '방학 때'처럼 시간 명사들은 'N 때'의 형태로 사용하고 상태나 동작을 표현하고 싶으면 현재 진행 중인 것은 '-을 때', 이미 끝난 것은 '-었을 때'로 표현한다.

40 십자가 *Cross*

Background Knowledge

윤동주의 집안은 1886년 함경북도에서 간도로 이주했고 1900년 명동촌에 정착하였다. 1910년에는 가족 모두가 기독교에 입교했는데 이 시에는 그러한 종교적 영향이 강하게 드러난다. 윤동주는 자신이 신앙하는 예수의 삶을 그대로 실천하려고 노력하였고 도덕적인 결단 앞에 망설이는 자신에 대해 끊임없이 반성하는 모습을 보였다. 예수가 본인의 죽음으로써 "서로 사랑해야 한다."는 진리를 회복했던 것처럼 윤동주도 한글로 시를 쓰는 십자가를 기꺼이 짊으로써 독립운동에 동참하고자 하였다.

V다면

어떤 가정된 사실을 조건으로 한다는 의미를 나타낼 때 쓰는 연결 어미이다. 다른 사람이 한 말을 전하는 간접 화법인 '-다고 하면'이 줄어든 말로 쓰이기도 한다. 동사 어간의 받침 유무 및 요청, 청유 여부에 따라 '-는다면/-ㄴ다면, -(으)라면, -자면'으로 바꾸어 쓴다.

41 간 Liver

Background Knowledge

〈토끼의 간〉 이야기와 〈프로메테우스〉 신화에는 공통적으로 '간'이 나온다. 〈토끼의 간〉에서 토끼는 거북이(자라)에게 속아서 용왕에게 간을 뺏기고 죽음을 당할 뻔하지만 거짓말로 위기를 벗어난다. 코카사쓰 산은 그리스 로마 신화에 등장하는 프로메테우스가 제우스를 속이고 인간에게 불을 훔쳐 준 죄로 벌을 받아 묶이게 된 산이다. 시인은 이 시의 배경을 코카사쓰 산으로 하고 토끼를 등장시켜서 두 이야기를 연결하였다.

AV어라

명령의 뜻을 나타내는 종결 어미이다. 모음 'ㅏ', 'ㅓ', 'ㅕ', 'ㅐ', 'ㅔ'로 끝나는 어간 뒤에는 '-라'만 붙여 쓰고, 동사 어간에 받침이 있을 때는 어간의 모음이 'ㅜ, ㅓ, ㅠ, ㅕ'이면 '-어라', 'ㅗ, ㅏ, ㅛ, ㅑ'이면 '-아라'를 쓴다. 'N하다' 동사는 'N해라'로 쓴다. 책 등의 시각 매체에서는 구체적으로 정해지지 않은 청자나 독자를 향하여 'AV(으)라'의 형태로 강한 요청의 뜻을 전달하기도 한다.

42 햇빛·바람 Sunlight·Wind

AV(으)려고

화자가 어떤 행동을 할 의도를 가지고 있음을 나타내는 연결 어미이다. 그러한 목적을 이루기 위해 필요한 행동이면 어떤 동사든지 이 어미 뒤에 이어서 등장할 수 있다. 하지만 이와 비슷하게 의도를 나타내는 어미로 'AV(으)러'가 있는데, 이 어미 뒤에는 '가다/오다'처럼 장소 이동을 나타내는 동사만 써야 한다.

43 츠르게네프의 언덕 Turgenev's Hill

N이나 AV

별로 마음에 들지 않지만 다른 방법이 없어서 할 수 없이 선택함을 나타내는 보조사이다. '굿이나 보고 떡이나 먹자.'와 같이 가장 좋은 것을 선택하면서도 그것이 제일 좋은 선택은 아닌 척하는 데 쓰기도 한다.

44 소년 The Boy

AV어/아 보다

어떤 행동을 시험 삼아 한다는 뜻을 나타내는 보조 동사이다.

45 위로 Comfort

V1어/아도 V2기만 하다

'-어/아도'는 가정이나 양보의 뜻을 나타내는 연결 어미이다. 후행절의 '-기만 하다'와 함께 써서 '어/아도' 앞에 쓰인 상황으로부터 예상되는 것과 반대되는 상황만이 후행절에 전개됨을 나타낸다. 후행절의 동사는 한 어절의 자동사인 경우가 자연스러우며 명사가 포함된 후행절이라면 'N만 하다'의 형태로 고쳐 쓰는 것이 자연스럽다.

46 병원 Hospital

Background Knowledge

윤동주가 연희전문학교를 다니던 시절에 세브란스 병원의 전신인 광혜원(1885)은 한국 최초의 서양식 병원이었다. 연희전문학교 캠퍼스 안에 위치한 이 병원의 환자들을 보며 윤동주는 그들의 고통에 크게 공감하였다. 윤동주는 당시 한반도 전체가 아픈 사람들로 가득하다고 생각하였기 때문에 자기 시집의 제목을 〈병원〉으로 지을까 고민했다고도 전해진다. 이 시가 지어진 1940년에 정병욱이 연희전문학교에 입학하여 1938년에 입학한 윤동주와 교유를 시작하게 된다. 이 해에 윤동주는 협성교회에 다니면서 영어 성서반에 들었고 외삼촌인 김약연 선생에게서 『시경』을 배웠다.

V도록

선행절의 내용이 후행절의 목적이나 결과, 방식, 정도가 됨을 나타내는 연결 어미이다. 시간을 나타내는 표현과 함께 쓰면 시간의 경과를 강조하는 의미가 생긴다. 시간에 따라 해야 할 일이 정해진 단체 안에서 특정한 시간에 기대하는 일이 이루어지지 않았을 때 걱정이나 섭섭함, 짜증 등 부정적인 심리가 생기는 것을 강조하는 데 쓰인다.

 무서운 시간
A Frightening Time

V(으)ㄹ 텐데

'V(으)ㄹ 텐데'는 'V(으)ㄹ 터인데'의 줄임말이다. '터'는 '예정'이나 '추측', '의지'의 뜻을 나타내는 의존 명사이며, '인데'와 결합하여 화자의 추측이나, 의지, 화자가 처한 상황에 대해 설명한다.

 쉽게 씌어진 시
A Poem Easily Written

Background Knowledge

윤동주는 릿교대학 유학 시절인 1942년 4-6월 동안 〈쉽게 씌어진 시〉 등 시 5편을 서울에 있는 친구 강처중에게 우편으로 보냈다. 이 시들은 오늘날 확인할 수 있는 그의 마지막 작품이다. 이로부터 1년 뒤인 1943년 7월 윤동주는 송몽규 등과 함께 일본 경찰에 체포됐고, 1944년 3월에 치안 유지법 위반으로 징역 2년형을 선고 받았다.

V는/은 줄 알면서도

'줄'은 어떤 방법이나 판단을 의미하는 의존 명사이다. '알다, 모르다'와 함께 쓰여서 화자의 배경지식의 정도를 나타낸다. '-면서도'는 '-면서'에 '도'가 붙은 형태로 선행절의 내용과 대조되는 행위가 후행절에 등장한다는 것을 나타낸다.

49 참회록 Confession

Background Knowledge

그는 편지지에 이 시를 쓰고 나서 5일 후에 일본 유학에 필요한 서류 작성을 위해 '히라누마(平沼) 도오주'로 창씨개명을 하였다.

N이면 N마다

'이면'은 둘 이상의 사물을 같은 자격으로 이어 주는 접속 조사이다. 이 조사 앞뒤로 같은 명사 혹은 유사한 범주의 명사 구절을 2개 이상 나열하고 '낱낱이 모두'라는 의미의 보조사 '마다'와 함께 쓰면 '(그러한 명사 혹은 명사구) 모두 다'라는 의미를 나타낸다. 동일한 명사를 반복 사용함으로써 긍정이나 부정적인 느낌을 강조하기도 한다.

50 별 헤는 밤
A Night Counting Stars

Background Knowledge

윤동주는 1941년 12월에 전쟁으로 인한 학기 단축 조치에 따라 예정보다 3개월 빠르게 연희전문학교를 졸업했다. 그리고 1942년 봄에 일본으로 유학을 떠나기에 앞서 자선 시집 『하늘과 바람과 별과 시』를 출간하려고 하였으나 돈이 없어서 그 뜻을 이루지 못했다. 그래서 자필 원고 3부를 만들어 한 부는 본인이, 한 부는 스승 이양하에게, 한 부는 후배 정병욱에게 남겼다. 이후에 정병욱은 1944년 1월에 전라남도 광양시에 계시던 어머니에게 '목숨처럼 소중한 것이니 잘 간직해 달라'라며 이 원고를 맡겼다. 그리고 이 정병욱이 맡긴 원고가 1946년 〈하늘과 바람과 별과 시〉로 출간되었다.

DV이/히

형용사 어간에 붙어서 형용사를 부사로 파생시키는 접사이다. '이'는 주로 명사나 'ㅂ 불규칙 동사' 뒤에 붙인다. '하다'를 붙여서 단어가 되는 경우 대개 '히'를 붙이는데 그 단어의 어근 받침이 'ㅅ'과 'ㄱ'인 경우는 예외적으로 '이'를 붙인다. 부사어는 그 부사가 꾸미는 동사의 바로 앞에 쓰는 것이 자연스럽다.

ㄱ

50 Poems
by Yoon Dong-ju
for Learners of
Korean

한국어 학습자를 위한 윤동주 시 50선

Written by	Kim Sungsook
Translated by	Jamie Lypka
First Published	September, 2025
First Printing	September, 2025
Publisher	Chung Kyudo
Editor-in-Chief	Lee Suk-hee
Editor	Lee Hyeon-soo
Cover design	Yoon Ji-Young
Interior design	Yoon Ji-Young, Yoon Hyun-ju
Illustrated by	Miho
Voice Actor	Kim In

 **DARAKWON** Published by Darakwon, Inc.

Darakwon Bldg., 210 Munbal-ro, Paju-si
Gyeonggi-do, Republic of Korea 10881
Tel : 02-736-2031 Fax : 02-732-2037
(Marketing Dept. ext.: 250~252, Editorial Dept. ext.: 420~426)

ISBN   978-89-277-3353-9 13710

http://www.darakwon.co.kr
http://koreanbooks.darakwon.co.kr

※ Visit the Darakwon homepage to learn about our other publications and promotions
and to download the contents in MP3 format.

50 Poems
by Yoon Dong-ju
for Learners of Korean

한국어 학습자를 위한 윤동주 시 50선

Kim Sungsook

Poetry Journal

50 Poems by Yoon Dong-ju for Learners of Korean

Poetry Journal

한국어 학습자를 위한 윤동주 시 50선

(01) 봄 1

우리 애기는

아래 발치에서 코올코올

고양이는

부뚜막에서 가릉가릉

애기 바람이

나뭇가지에 소올소올

아저씨 햇님이

하늘 한가운데서 째앵째앵

02 못 자는 밤

03 무얼 먹고 사나

04 나무

05 산울림

06 식권

07 병아리

⟨08⟩ 가슴 3

09 할아버지

(10) 호주머니

11 개 1

12 오줌싸개 지도

13 이불

(14) 그 여자

15 해바라기 얼굴

(16) 가슴 2

17 반딧불

⑱ 산협의 오후

19 고향집 – 만주에서 부른

20 새로운 길

21 귀뚜라미와 나와

(22) 바람이 불어

23 비둘

24 사과

25 슬픈 족속

(26) 서시

27 참새

(28) 남쪽 하늘

(29) 밤

30 눈 감고 간다

31 새벽이 올 때까지

(32) 비행기

(33) 창구멍

34 유언

35 아우의 인상화

(36) 사랑스런 추억

37 코스모스

자화상

간판 없는 거리

십자가

41 간

42 햇빛 · 바람

햇빛 · 바람

츠르게네프의 언덕

 위로

병원

47 무서운 시간

(48) 쉽게 씌어진 시

49 참회록

50 별 헤는 밤

50 Poems
by Yoon Dong-ju
for Learners of
Korean

한국인 학습자를 위한 윤동주 시 50선

Poetry Journal

Written by	Kim Sungsook
Translated by	Jamie Lypka
First Published	September, 2025
First Printing	September, 2025
Publisher	Chung Kyudo
Editor-in-Chief	Lee Suk-hee
Editor	Lee Hyeon-soo
Cover design	Yoon Ji-Young
Interior design	Yoon Ji-Young, Yoon Hyun-ju
Illustrated by	Miho
Voice Actor	Kim In

DARAKWON Published by Darakwon, Inc.

Darakwon Bldg., 210 Munbal-ro, Paju-si
Gyeonggi-do, Republic of Korea 10881
Tel : 02-736-2031 Fax : 02-732-2037
(Marketing Dept. ext.: 250~252, Editorial Dept. ext.: 420~426)

ISBN 978-89-277-3353-9 13710

---

http://www.darakwon.co.kr
http://koreanbooks.darakwon.co.kr

※ Visit the Darakwon homepage to learn about our other publications and promotions
and to download the contents in MP3 format.

50 Poems
by Yoon Dong-ju
for Learners of Korean

Poetry Journal

한국어 학습자를 위한 윤동주 시 50선